Modern Civilization

by the Same Author

1. *Stone Age Industries of the Bombay and Satara Districts*
2. *Indian Civilization: The Formative Period (A Study of Archaeology as Anthropology)*
3. *Understanding Indian Civilization: A Framework of Enquiry*
4. *Indian Civilization: The First Phase (Problems of a Source Book)*
5. *Dissent, Protest and Reform Movements in Indian Civilization*
6. *Indian Movements: Some Aspects of Dissent, Protest and Reform*
7. *Criteria of Social Status in India*
8. *Determinants of Social Status in India*
9. *Management and Organization of Indian Universities*

Modern Civilization

A Crisis of Fragmentation

S.C. Malik

DK PRINTWORLD
Publishers of Indian Traditions

Cataloging in Publication Data — DK
[Courtesy: D.K. Agencies (P) Ltd. <docinfo@dkagencies.com>]

Malik, S. C. (Subhash Chandra), 1932- **author.**
Modern civilization : a crisis of fragmentation / S.C. Malik. – Revised and enlarged edition.
pages cm
"First published in India in 1989" – Title page verso.
Includes bibliographical references and index.
ISBN 9788124610299 (HB)

1. Civilization – Philosophy. I. Title.

LCC CB19.M35 2020 | DDC 901 23

ISBN: 978-81-246-1029-9
First published in India in 1989
Revised and enlarged edition published in 2020

Printed and published by:
D.K. Printworld (P) Ltd.
Regd. Office: "Vedasri", F-395, Sudarshan Park
(Metro Station: ESI Hospital) New Delhi - 110015
Phones: (011) 2545 3975; 2546 6019; Fax: (011) 2546 5926
e-mail: indology@dkprintworld.com
Website: www.dkprintworld.com

For

Anjali

Endorsements

Perhaps, one day the present consciousness would become so unbearable that it would spontaneously embark on a totally new pattern. There are signs of that already; one of them is Malik's book. ... – *IIC Quarterly*, 1990

This book is for the discerning reader, lay as well as academic. If you are not then save yourself, the time and money. Or buy yet another book that makes you reach for the bottle. ...

– *India Magazine*, 1990

This is a book which does make a number of interesting challenges, the sharpest blows being reserved for thought per se. ...

– *Times of India*, 1991

... merit lies in bringing the importance of incorporating the Asian wisdom in the process of modernization which is dominated by Western outlook in life. – *Anthropos*, Germany, 1991

He definitely given food for thought to any reader in touch with the source of one's existential experimental dimension.

– *Hindu*, 1990

This is a fascinating book. It should be read with great profit by our scientific technocratic managerial life.

– *Indian Horizons*, 1990

... work is a creative and thoughtful addendum to Tagore's explication of the concept of civilization. ... – *Vishvabharati Qly*, 1990

... a worthwhile addition to the whole range of recent publications both in the field of natural and the social sciences, philosophy and even art history. ... – *Mainstream*, 1990

... is a remedial analysis of the contemporary intellectual and cultural imbalance in the world ... it moves skilfully from Western to Eastern thinking ... the analysis of the empirical experience of the mind is cleverly executed, and the concluding ideas do appear in a context where a Western reader should find them comprehensible ... the value and impressive range of Dr. Malik's analysis. ...

– Peter Malekin, in *Temenos*, 13, 1992

... the importance, I would venture to say, in the fact that it is, more anthropological than others (dealing with modern crisis of man) ... observes modern civilization both from within and without ... some affinities between the general approach of S.C. Malik and the general movement of cognitive research, whose magnitude is know to all today. ... Four themes particularly seem to me deserving attention ... introspection, cultural relativism, cognitive research, normative element in the modes of knowledge ... certain propositions are debatable ... he is performing the functions of a philosopher ... not a moralist ... its importance lies in the planetary nature of the questions raised ... his book belongs to the family of those who demonstrate most vividly this "outdatedness", each in his particular style.

– Review Article by J.C. Gardin in *L'Homme*, Paris, 1993

... we have heard this before; but here it is especially telling that the critique of myopic specialization and exploitation comes from beyond the West itself and is especially compelling to hear the urgent call for the reintegration expressed in a fresh accent ... sympathetic readers are amply rewarded.

– *Comparative Studies in History and Society*, Camb. 1991

... you had traced a path that led me through somehow familiar regions ... to the very point poetry had led me ... I did think catch a glimpse of how consciousness itself is reality ... thankyou for having led me by your forest-path to a long-sought and very familiar place ... your analysis of the unquestioned premises ... is quite brilliant and of course deadly aceurate ... also impressed ... about Man as the Microcosm. I felt increasing recognition of the path you were making and where it was leading the reader, I felt as if you were leading an initiate into the Mysteries, whose final realization is that we had known it all the time. ...

– Kathaleen Raine (1991 Letter)

... He delves deeply into the ... emergency ... provokes the thoughtful reader to a serious engagement with his or her self by his novel way of thinking. ... – *Mountain Path*, 1991

... Malik's account of the crisis of contemporary civilization can hardly be contested and reading him one becomes aware of the need to reawaken our humanity and change our framework of values. – *New Quest*, 1991

... It is a stern warning. The author emphasizes the urgent need for self-discovery and total awareness, a complete inward transformation of the individual psyche ... a quest for wholeness and a retrieval of the lost harmony. – *The Theosophist*, 1991

Here is a fascinating book on modern civilization ... is able to provoke the reader's interest in the "crisis of fragmentation" that modern civilization is facing. – *Contributions to Indian Sociology*, 1991

This insightful and challenging book takes the reader to question the paradigms of "progress", both individual and collective, when one normally takes them for granted. With its enlightened perspective on human existence, it urges one to know one-self in order to save all. – *Indian Book Chronicle*, 1992

The author keeps largely to human experience on earth and its widest and deepest potential for creativity. He does not venture into speculative areas. Goethe has, cryptically put this issue in just one sentence. If you want to stride into the infinite, just walk to all sides of the finite. – *Indian and World Arts and Crafts*, 1991

His logical argument and his never failing insight (and excellent quality) ... sustained rigorously throughout the book, is admirable. Scholars of philosophy, mysticism, and civilization studies will find the book very useful. ... – *Asian Fhilosophy*, U.K., 1993

... insightful book ... brings into question ... this age-old Western value and bias about activity and contemplation ... the alienation of the inner self from the outer self ... what Malik is saying is very vital; it needs to be heard by scholars everywhere. ... Malik's words and observations are wise and daring ... needs to be listened to ... where the material well-being is not seen as the "end of history" ... is pleading for ... a continuing search for alternatives to the prevailing ideas of development, and the meaning and values of life. – *Environments*, Canada, 1993

Preface to the Second Edition

TODAY the crisis of modern civilization is in a very precarious state since this book was first published in 1989. Fragmentation is getting worse at all levels: political, economic, social, cultural and, most importantly, at psychological level. The binary divisions mentioned in the first edition, say domination vs subordination, man vs nature, self vs the other, you vs me, self vs society, and so on, are so much accentuated that the very existence of not only humankind but all of nature and in fact the very existence of the earth is on the way to extinction. Entropy has set in.

Very little attention is being given to this disorder in the brain itself, as all attention is focused on the externals and very little to any inward movement in order to understand the movement of the mind, and to such crucial question as "who am I?". This psychological disease is not being addressed as to what causes this crisis of fragmentation of modern humankind. All solutions are directed to the external conditions, misleadingly labelled as "progress", "development" and so on, *sans* human face, and focused within the concept of linear time. Critically these concepts have been reduced to technological and commercial (consumerism) "growth" as indicators. This overemphasis is at the expense of even Nature, which is at the receiving end of all man-made disasters. Man is the only species that kills its own kind which no other species has done so far, and that too by killing millions, and is using warfare as a means to make profit. Most of all it is being used in the outdated concept of nations or nationalism, controlled by the industrial–military complex run by the corporates under the garb of political governance. All these enterprises and concepts continue to dominate modern civilizations with their outdated and outmoded notions, to repeat within linear time and binary divisions in opposition rather than living in cooperation.

In short, in the context of the brain which is in disorder since the left analytical brain hemisphere dominates. This is at the expense of the right hemisphere which has the intuitive brain that sees the world holistically and is the domain of love, beauty, compassion, sharing and caring via experientially, having an insight. This creative domain produces painting, music, poetry, non-verbal manifestation, oral history and such manifestations, storytelling and narratives wherein they are a participatory community and a participatory universe as well.

In the absence of coordination and cooperation between two spheres – say the metaphor of Yin and Yang or Śiva and Pārvatī, etc. – that all destructive movement is happening and it is obvious in climate change expressing itself in all the violence that we see all around. This had its beginning psychologically. Clearly, in this disorder there are no signs of even any moral indigination as integrity and authenticity are absent, which are the core features a human being. That is why all relationships are transactional in nature, there is no faith or trust any longer.

In other words, the crisis is a psychological disorder, and as Gandhiji had summed it up: "There is enough for one's need but not enough for one's greed."

These crucial issues, which were seriously addressed in the earlier edition, are still valid today, provided one cares to read the book seriously. The earlier diagrams have been elaborated and described afresh in the text and hopefully will help the reader in understanding the main emphasis of the book.

I am grateful to Shri Susheel Mittal of D.K. Printworld who has taken a bold decision to bring out this new edition.

New Delhi **S.C. Malik**
29 December 2019

Preface to the First Edition

THERE is little doubt that at the back of a discussion of the crisis facing mankind today, there is also, broadly speaking, the search for the lost harmony. Many serious investigative, expressive and creative endeavours are apparently being made towards the fulfilment of this goal. These efforts may further be categorized as intellectual, artistic, scientific and so on. Fundamentally these attempts may be said to be towards rediscovering one's place in the scheme of things. But are these attempts in the right direction, i.e. these are good enough to usher in the reign of peace? Are even the reasons for these kinds of endeavours, individually or collectively, correctly formulated? Does this rethinking only arise out of some a priori and socially conditioned metaphysical assumption, as the existence of misery, suffering, widespread unhappiness, or is there really an earnestness to recreate, revitalize and formulate radically new metaphysical truths in consonance with the present crisis? At any rate, all these efforts reflect a general dissatisfaction with the way life is today, as is so obvious from notable events the world over. This indicates a "crisis" period, a moment when mankind has the intense desire to re-establish a harmonious relationship between one's self and the other, between nature and man, etc.

There is the too obvious threat of a nuclear war, the War to end all wars. In passing it may also be mentioned that more, and deadlier, weapons have been used after, than in the last world war, and that they continue to take their toll. The shape of World War III may be like this since all the superpowers are involved albeit it is not labelled as World War III because these wars are not on the territories of the superpowers. At any rate, nuclear wastes and the pollution of a global nature are causing such ecological imbalances that pose a threat to the extinction of man, and perhaps to all life on this planet. But must mankind survive — does it deserve to — considering the fact that it has destroyed many millions of species, including its own kind?

At any rate, if all through the earlier part of the twentieth century the practical results of scientific and technological developments were a great boon — especially sometime soon after World War II and the then buoyant mood — today the same mood has turned into a crisis of confidence. The way of progress, often equated with high technology, has led modern social and political systems to inflict barbarous inhumanities, unprecedented in human history. These routine outrages now touch every section of humanity. This and all the other symptoms of the crisis make it imperative for one to explore and question the implications of those central perceptions and fundamental paradigms of reality which govern most of "modern" mankind, that is, linear time and sequential causation, materialism, rationalism, the separation of mind from matter, of man from nature, individual vs society, objectivity vs subjectivity, many other similar notions of binary oppositions (confrontation dualities), and so on (Papadopoullos 1975). Thus, for in actual fact we continue to date to be governed by an intellectual comprehension of the material world which we understand to be composed of separate objects or particles. While the subscription to the concept has allowed man to dominate both inanimate and animate nature, strife and domination within humanity itself is also the result of such a simplistic philosophy, "domination vs subordination", a continuation of man's early struggles on the planet. We also continue to believe that sheer quantitative accumulation of information will somehow reveal the secret of the universe. It is increasingly being realized — by some if not many — that this is a shortsighted prescription minus any vision of long-term consequences for the globe. We are paying dearly for living in a self-wrought ignorance, despite warnings from many quarters. Their's is the warning, that the principle on which we have built our so-called present civilization is suspect. The voices from within the scientific community are equally vocal, as in the know, as these are of principles which issue from an understanding of physics, biology, chemistry, psychology, holistic medicine and so on (Dossey 1982).

Apparently, there is at the moment a deep-seated apathy, conservatism or lethargy in the spirit of man. In order to shake ourselves out of such impasse what is required of us as a first step is the reconsideration of our fundamental suppositions wherein lies the seat of our contemporary malaise. While there are many apparent factors for such a state of affairs, there are two interrelated factors which may be considered of special significance.

1. The value placed on specialization or segmentation. This procedure, beginning at the level of thought, is then extended to our observation of the external world and its categorization. But in the process, the total view is obscured. For this shortcoming, there are good reasons. To give but one example, the structural form of bureaucracy is absolutely opposed to any kind of holism or holistic thinking. Even scientific education nurses the belief that specialization will by itself unravel the mystery of the universe. But the continuation of a narrow, one-sided vision such as this has further secured, and so at all levels, those vested interests as have become utterly ill-adapted to reconsider the fundamentals. The motive of conservatism is not to sustain the endeavours for truth — which in effect means continuously discarding, outmoded conclusions and research methodologies — it is to continue operating in small compartments of learning. It is this very perspective that continues to keep intact a situation of conflict and tension, disregarding not only the respect for truth but even the welfare of humanity and the health of the environment at large. Fragmentation is in fact an issue, of far-reaching implication in the structure of the brain itself that is creating psychological disorder, since techno-scientific developments are neutral in themselves. Duality and over-specialization between them have caused untold havoc in present mankind's socio-psychic being.
2. Being caught up in an ever-narrowing circle of vision, not many serious attempts for alternate world views have been

made yet. This is true the world over, though perhaps less so in the West. But still most developing societies continue to be fed on an outdated philosophy which ignores outright several indigenous view points and perceptions. In fact, in the process of modernization there has been a systematic mental obliteration of any alternative as may have already been available in the past. Moreover, this same obliviousness makes for the destruction of other life forms beyond the need of survival and for a handful to dominate the less technologically developed or underprivileged peoples. Technological development and "progress" have no limits to territorial ambition. For instance, in India, the same unthinking bureaucratic structures, following outdated conceptual models of the nineteenth-century Europe and the concomitant industry and technology, are being imposed into the interior rural and village societies. There are also judgements on cultural differences, so that the communication media (newspapers, radio, television, etc.), even with all good intentions such as national integration, are erasing human cultural variety as have been an outgrowth of the spontaneous and natural response of a society to its environment and psychic being. There seems to be an inherent belief, by and large, that development of science and technology is the one sure sign of progress; that it is the only means that gives clear access to the understanding of nature. This widespread belief, even though it is now being counteracted by science in the West itself, is yet widely prevalent.

Thus, in counting the leaves, the overall view of the tree seems to have been completely overlooked. Actually the fundamentals of science are not opposed to the knowledge that arises from religious or other modes of perception. Science, as applied to human affairs and which policymakers seem to understand in a superficial way, has become the only possibility of our perception and construction of reality. It is little realized that this is only a sketch map to one aspect of the cosmos, not the whole of it. We may acknowledge Einstein, who clearly states that scientific laws are merely patterns we impose upon reality, in order to make sense of it by means of simplification. Because, otherwise, the universe in its inconceivable vastness threatens to overwhelm the limited capacity of our organism to comprehend it. But, if we take this limited way of organizing knowledge to be "reality", then shall we not be blind to the potential solutions to our problems which many other earlier, or currently restated world views of disparate civilizations may have to offer? "As far as the laws of mathematics refer to reality, they are not certain and as far as they are certain, they do not refer to reality", said Einstein. Hence, the mechanical life is a kind of unimaginative thinking, one that has cut-off man from his existential–experiential source of being.

Most of what has been stated above is known. However it is interesting to note that there is many a Western poet, philosopher or mystic who has felt at odds with the cultural implications of modern science and technology. Hence, the contemporary malaise of mankind is not unoften called a "spiritual crisis". This situation is not restricted to the West alone. We may now use the word "Western" to imply a world view (in favour of the new technological civilization, "progress", etc.) which is prevalent in any geographical or political zone. For example, a large number of "Westerners" continue to dominate Indian polity and economy in imposing an alternative future, without taking into account the psyche of the cultural configuration or civilization, called India (Malik 1978a). Surprisingly, mechanistic techno-economic models, linked to progress and development, are deemed to be the only indicators of modern life.

Despite some dissidence on an individual plane, there is little serious challenge to these assumptions from any reckonable quarters — the science faculties, or the liberal, democratic institutions. It cannot therefore be denied that these same models have a hegemony which remains unchallenged by and large. It is in this wider context that there has been a surgical transplant of superficial or pseudo-science and technology in India — with all the covert assumptions of domination and exploitation — spreading into the sociocultural milieu very subtly, and in the process subverting all that is indigenous and unique to the Indian tradition in the deeper sense. We may therefore say that there is a lack of integration of the new science and technology with the rest of Indian culture, but which culture had once upon a time its own scientific rational tradition, albeit in some ways with different aspirations.

This critique is however not a call to ignore modern science and technology. Far from it. It has been undertaken to note how we are helplessly bound, especially in educational and bureaucratic systems, by a kind of what may be termed unhealthy epistemological imperialism. While the modern mind is one and the same the world over, it is no longer integrated with what we may call the heart. For this very reason the future lies in peril, for the whole of mankind. Truth is, the developing nations cannot depend upon technological blueprints and models transplanted from other areas. To illustrate (while being conversant with all that the West has to offer), we may take into account the philosophical category of Beingness. Now, if we term the present Western being as external and the Eastern as internal, the harmonization of the two alone will allow the full development of man's potentialities. Such qualitative integration is the need of the time. Both paths are in pursuit of the truth, though today, erroneously, going divergently in opposition to each other. In short, much of the mankind of today is leading a truncated life — a separation of the mind from the heart.

It may easily be construed with regard to what has been stated above, that the idea of progress, in order to bring about a change, should be avoided since it is based on a narrow or functional rationality of science and technology. This inhibition too surfaced in the West, and where there is considerable anti-evolutionary, anti-rational and anti-progress movement at the moment. But this has come to pass, as a reaction to the excess of affluence. But an anti-rational movement, at this juncture for the rest of the world, may merely reinforce extreme forms of irrationalism, obscurantism and other negative philosophies which themselves perpetuate injustices, inequalities and so forth. The movement from abject poverty and misery to a certain basic human standards, of living, to egalitarianism — and which is a must — requires an affirmative philosophy through a balancing of world views, obviously for which socio-economics forms the foundation. The internalization of values of such ideas is not in contradiction to any traditional goals in spirit, though not in the way the latter have tended to become dogmas.

The votaries of modernization need to bear in mind indigenous paradigms and patterns. This is why outside models do need to be carefully screened, in order that no abstract model may be imposed on the rich variety and diversity of cultures and societies that exist on the planet. The idea of human progress, through man's own choosing, effort, may well resurface through other already existing, even though presently lying dormant, as cultural core values. This however is not be construed as an advocacy for the prevailing dogmatic or almost fatalistically deterministic sectarian philosophies (Malik 1971a). The reference is to those universal values which in the final analysis are common to all of humankind, i.e. freedom of spirit and the happiness in joy, values that lie in the very recesses of man's being.

Thus, both cultural relativity and being free from the idea of relativity (so far as the universalization of certain common human values are concerned) have to take place. These values are no new thing, for the higher religion and the science in their fundamental assumptions have stated the same. In this day and age of specialization, the need of the hour is a return to reflection and synthesis. Knowledge, both practical and theoretical — if it is divorced from the deeper thought, speculation, imagination or vision — is of little worth. The need is a coherent philosophy, one which includes man's relationship not only with the plants and animals, but with the earth as a part of the human universe. A radical psychological transformation in human consciousness itself is imperative, as much as a socio-economic revolution. Fragmentation and separation have caused the alienation of man from his inner Being. This in turn causes the contemporary crisis of a catastrophic magnitude. Since the basic paradigm of dualities, say "individual vs the world", operates in all spheres of life and is a way whereby thought perpetuates itself, can it create world unity, universal value systems or harmony? Can a mind divided within — thought in contradiction and conflict — discover totality, despite such well-intentioned efforts?

Man as a species has specialized in the development of thought, by making symbols and images of experiences that are recorded as memory. In the past, this certainly helped to anticipate the future, as deduced from the experiences of the past. This power betokened a great advantage over the animal world in the early stages of evolution, but soon the same power was in time used as a mean to dominate other cultural groups. This development of a fragment of the brain, meant for human survival in the early stages, is overspecialized in its functioning even when this is not necessary. Instead of the survival of the individual and the groups, it has made its own survival imperative, i.e. that mechanical repetitive ideas by themselves have become important, often unrelated to any functional experiential advantage. That man has enough weapons to kill his kind fifty times over — as if once were not enough — is a comment on the state of affairs. It underlines the domination of idea and ideology at the cost of man himself. In other words, mechanical thought — as described — rides man. of course, it is necessary to have thought as an instrument, it is *via-media* or a technology which was created for man. But now it dominates its own creator. It is thought — as matter, as mechanical technology — which is the crux of the problem. In other words, today, the symbols, expressions and interpretations of the experiential dimension are taken to be more real. Those are what are confused with feelings and are repeated mechanically through reified formulas or rituals. One overlooks that thought is an interpretation, the view point of a given experience, but not the experience, not actuality itself. But all of us, as persons, identify with thought as if the beliefs, judgements, conclusions are our identity, our life. Thought moves — if we are acutely aware, choicelessly notice — from "what was" to "what should be", a pendualm movement that misses the present, the now of life.

The cortex will be in a chaos, when partially functioning, in an overspecialized manner, as a fragment. So it can deteriorate or be dormant for a lack of use. There may be an imbalance when its total functioning is in abeyance. Here is a fundamental problem from which project such individual and social issues which humankind is at present discussing. Functioning in a limited sphere thought contradicts itself, i.e. what it says and what it does — this being the basic disorder. Mankind continues to live in an outdated paradigm of dichotomies, of "survival", e.g. "you vs me", "body vs mind", "individual vs collectivity", "East vs West", "religion vs science" and so on. One can well imagine what could happen to an instrument suffering from contradiction or conflict and also running in two directions! Will it not, in doing this be neurotic, have a split personality? What new beginnings can be made, given a situation such as this?

But take another example of the disordered functioning of the brain. For all of us a good night's sleep is one when we completely forget all activities that took place during the day, including one's own name, even one's own body, or those various relationships which we consider as crucial when awake. This is what is called a good refreshing sleep especially when the mind's chatter stops. But the moment we are awake the chatter begins anew and one is doing everything to enhance, that "I" which sees advantage; all the other similar goals built in the social system. But even in a case like this, people often take to various addictions or anodynes in order to quieten the restless mind. In fact, man is ever seeking — through his will to achievement — that quality which produces a kind of communion. He seeks moments of silence and peace as takes place in any aesthetic experience, of seeing the beauty of a flower, a mountain, or being near the sea.

Thus the mind is moving in two directions at the same time: one which enhances the self through the instrumentality of thought, and the second via which everything is erased in order to receive peace. Of course, when one is totally immersed in action, there is no separate thought or "I". The "I" is a psychosomatic construct amidst an aggregate of thoughts, i.e. the thinker is the thought. But this situation creates several selves: subjectivity referring itself through various pronouns and having a dialogue within and without by creating the opposite or the other. It even does this, while trying to be altruistic and by destroying itself, in order to be free. In short, thought — in the given context — becomes a policeman as well as a thief at one and the same time. Given such a situation the human person once again seeks peace and harmony, as also tries to solve outer problems. But can one do so? Can any one succeed in understanding the world wearing coloured glasses (unaware in this conditioned set-up that it is viewing the world in this manner), see *what is*, or that which is actual? Can a conceptual self glimpse the real?

The presumption of social conditioning is that there is a "self", as a separate enduring entity, and that there are others. But is this true? For a moment let us examine the individual who is identified with his body. This body is made up of all the organic and inorganic elements, and it not being a mere product of one's lineage. Even one's name has been received through the social system with a long historical past through the social system. In other words, and to say the obvious, one is the product both in name and form of all the elements of the earth (which in turn being connected to the solar system, the galaxies, etc.), and the entire human sociocultural history. One may say that *the world is me* or *I am the world.*

Even if one may ask: what was I before this name and form came into existence? What was born, did it happen through my will? If so, what was I before or did I have any choice in the name and form already given? Even the death of the body is already programmed. This is a no choice situation, then what is this *me* that one refers to? Similarly the process of thinking and thought which one considers as one's own: can one stop thought or start it? There is no choice in the given situation, i.e. when you identify with who you think you are. It might be useful to reflect on these questions of how much one really knows oneself, and considers oneself to be having a will, or to be the doer? Question is, can a restless instrument see clearly, can a grimy mirror reflect truly?

The self-conscious I or ego is always incomplete and as "such" selfish, with surfeit of other negative qualities. But beyond who one thinks one is, i.e. as a conceptual self, who am I? Everything takes place because consciousness is primordial, for this is what makes us aware of all that we are talking about, and because without it nothing will be possible. So who I am is this very consciousness, this insight and intelligence which is the context within which everything else takes place. But this consciousness is not yours or mine. You and I are in consciousness, this is one's Beingness. It is this Beingness which allows the experiencing, the process of life. Experiencing and witnessing consciousness creates the experiencer and the experienced, secondarily. The experiencer and the experienced are one and the same thing. Beingness is all that there is common to us irrespective of all the other categories superimposed on it. It is like the surface waves of the ocean with which we identify as if these were separate from the ocean.

Actually, and in the context we are speaking, there is no "you" and "me"; these are only conceptual and provisional psychosomatic entities. The knowing–perceiving awareness is the principle, the process, which allows for everything to take place. This totality, wholeness and completeness is something which we experience as love in rare moments. During these moments, there is no concept of either time or space, as these are eternal moments of Now. Even when we speak of the past or the future, we only know it in the Now; we cannot see the past or future actually. On these eternal moments arise surface movements of the conceptual universe. But our lives are governed by an inverse understanding, i.e. the universe is real, and the eternal is conceptual. In fact, it is all One Whole.

Thus it is clear that all we need to do is to clearly see the misconceptions and clarify blurred notions. Seeing that one's point of view as the only reality is causing problems. This is what creates the dualistic paradigm of confrontation in all walks of life, that is precisely what needs to be changed. The transformation that one speaks about is a transformation of the perspective. For example, a Newtonian universe became an Einsteinian universe by a mere change of perspective. Everything exists already in the implicate order as potentialities. Both academically and otherwise, today we need the paradigm of complementarity, simultaneity and continuity. That alone may bring about the beginnings of alternate dimensions that we are seeking.

Thus, and to recapitulate, it is clear that the first step towards a mutation in the consciousness of mankind would be the coming of an experiential or holistic awareness. In its absence, the frustration and futility are likely to perpetuate themselves and very naturally so. It is not technology, which has produced enormous tools for food and other goods, nor scientific growth which is the cause of the present dilemma. It is the *causal notion* itself — of cause–effect relationship — that is at the very root of linear thought. Repetitive technology of imitative mechanical thought orientation — of certain memories — perpetuates itself by being "rational", in giving explanations and so on. Superficial dual thought, of course, has a function in day-to-day activities. It was also a critical development at the level of survival, at a time when mankind was in dire need of it against predators. Rapid civilizational growth took place with language, writing and so on. But mechanical thought (*there is also non-dual or deep thought*) is a kind of material technology which has become extremely specialized. Not only this, it has formed itself into a personal socio-psychological self or "ego" which in turn becomes whatever it identifies with as an idea. The essential survival mechanisms arose in a small area of the brain which has by now become hyperspecialized, leading to a risky fragmentation. This overdevelopment has caused the deadening of a large part of the brain. This overuse of the fractional brain, in fact, makes most of humankind subhuman. The physical brain as such may have already deteriorated considerably. Perhaps is this very condition causing evolutionary fatigue, a genetic depression, an entropy?

Evolutionarily speaking, it is given to us to choose *now*, to concomittantly bring about — along with science and technology — a radical psychological transformation. It is given to us to rehabilitate ourselves, simply by, foremost, being aware of this fragmentation, of this outmoded conditioning. This awareness itself is a change in the perspective that will lead to a transformation of the world, not vice versa. If most of those who control human society, including scholars and intellectuals, change (perhaps too many at present are totally unaware of this fundamental malaise), then only will the human mind which projects a disordered society outside create a transformed civilization. The awareness is not to be merely — though also necessary — intellectual, it has to be known through an individual experiential state as well. The organic view of life is, therefore, the imperative need of the day.

It is conceivable that the subtlest thought, the numerous encounters of the mind are also similarly registered like the genetic code, that has helped to revive and refashion each generation. But we know little of that level of thought, its functioning and its laws. As has been suggested by some there may be a common memory pool, functioning within a morphogenetic field. These are realms into which knowledge as available today — given its limited paradigm — can have little access to. The existing sociocultural or thought structures have depressed genetic matter so much that the accumulated knowledge of which modern man is so proud of has, in fact, become a hindrance. The world it creates and causes us to believe to be a *reality* is actually unreal. It is a projection of an unoriented mind which is not "true" to thinking about itself. Thus what we call the normal course of life is no longer a natural flow. Mankind has lost its naturalness and its spontaneity. The so-called "search for truth" is really a non-search. Since we are unable even to see *what is* the actual directly and perceptibly any longer, even true communication and true creativity learning is almost totally absent in human existence today.

Finally, it is important to understand the unit, the individual — the Whole, the One — within whom "everything and nothing" of the universe is contained. It is the knowledge of this unit which allows one to know instantly, intuitively and insightwise. This clarity is what effects everything else and will, no doubt, bring about a mutation in human consciousness. Fundamentally, all that is required is a transformation of the individual. There is no separation of civilizational crisis from individual crisis. *Who we are* is already whole and complete, not *who we think* we are. All this implies rethinking about culture, i.e. since culture implies a way of life. Is it not that the cultural paradigm itself has to be radically transformed?

A transformation, which will clear the crisis both of the individual and civilization, and the destruction towards which they are heading today, requires an awareness of what has been enumerated. While a change in awareness has been enjoined from times immemorial in various ancient texts of all religions in different means of self-expression, the prescription needs to be reiterated and restated. But it cannot remain within a mere theoretical or conceptual proposition, i.e. merely discussed, as with other things, at a superficial level. It is almost as if everybody theoretically speaks about the need to breathe, or states that once he knows what it is to breathe he can continue to operate theoretically. But as anybody knows there is no theoretical way of breathing for breathing in the right manner also has to be carried on moment to moment. This perspective has to be seen both intellectually and intuitively, insightwise.

The crisis facing mankind is of the same magnitude and urgency as that of breathing, or of putting one's hand into the fire of a burning house or any other urgency which makes any individual act instantly since there is no time or space for discussion. If the hand is burning the action is to immediately withdraw it, rather than having a discussion over it, or if one's house is on fire there is no time to discuss problems about water or the colour of the bucket and so on. Obvious though this may seem, yet it is equally apparent that such knowledge has not hit the right mark, or has not brought about sufficient misery and suffering for individuals in all spheres of life to take the necessary creative and corrective instant action. The game of being the victim, or else of blame and guilt, and of a discussion of these various dimensions continue to be operative in all walks of life of the individuals and it is these individuals who contribute to the totality of human civilization, for civilization by itself is an abstraction and the individual is an essential ingredient, its maker. As stated elsewhere each one affects, and is effected by the other and everything in the universe impinges upon everything else in order for anything to take place at any moment of time. It is, as has been said often, the drop of water contributes to the ocean and the ocean is in the drop itself.

In this sense, every part of the universe is of significance and contributes equally to its complete functioning provided the awareness is there of the whole context and not that of separate isolated entities or fragments. Many of the statements of ancient seers are being studied in the modern context of physics through both experiments and intuitive insights, i.e. of the essence of the seers are being studied in the modern context of physics through both experiments and intuitive insights, i.e. of the essence of the whole or the wholeness in parts which is essential for the totality to function the way it does. At any rate, this kind of self-awareness and attention of the functioning of consciousness and the mind whereby one learns and communicate is the fundamental dimension of true knowledge (*vidyā*), as against the illusion of separate individuals in which one believes in what has been labelled as ignorance (*avidyā*). This very awareness of falsehood of one's perspective, of the duality in which one functions, is the transformation that takes place instantly and becomes operative in all walks of life, by itself.

In other words, the removal of the dark glasses, the perspective itself, is the doing; there is no gap between perception and action at all. This is what is meant by instant action, and it becomes operative instantly and effects the functioning of the universe in the same way that ripples travel across when a stone is thrown in a pool of water. Thus the transformation of the individual is the beginning of transformation of the human civilization.

In Zen Buddhism there is a story about a Zen master who claimed that he could bring about enlightenment instantly. So a man who was very keen went to this Zen master, who took him in his eagerness to a nearby pool and asked him to look at his reflection closely by bending down. The moment he did so the Zen master got hold of his neck and put his head under water.

The man was for a moment intrigued and thought that "certainly before I have any problems of breathing there must be some instant way of getting enlightenment!" But when the Zen master did not allow him to take out his head from under water the man began to be worried since he could not hold his breath any longer. Nevertheless he thought that he will now definitely be enlightened. Finally, when he just could not bear not to breathe, the man with all his strength at his disposal got his head out of water and took a deep breath to fill his lungs. It is then that the Zen master said: "If you are keen on enlightenment your desire should be so forceful as your desire to breathe fully again." The desire has to be very strong and at this very instant if the individual and civilization, which **is** covered by ominous clouds of destruction and despair, wants truly to free itself of the crisis of fragmentation.

This monograph discusses many of these various well-known issues for stimulating a rethinking about a fateful contemporary dilemma. This is why the format of this monograph is not framed in terms of available current humanities and social science academic concepts and methodologies. At some point in the end the proposition and thesis will negate their own existence. Perhaps, this is the paradox which faces one who writes about experiential states; it cannot be understood especially within the framework of currently available academic writing. Nevertheless, it is perhaps the logical outcome of a long career in archaeology, history, anthropology within the context of civilizational studies, formulating models and conceptual frameworks. Perhaps, all this research was a search for explanations of my own existence. It is a realization that the seeker is the sought, and that a scholar has to move beyond his own limited conditioning of narrow boundaries. One hopes that it gives food for thought not only to academics but also to others, and the one in touch with the source of one's existential, experiential dimension that will allow mankind to be fully human.

Shimla **S.C. Malik**
Summer 1986

Contents

Acknowledgements

IT WAS at the Indian Institute of Advanced Study, Shimla, that this monograph was conceived and written; I am grateful for the opportunity provided, albeit it decided not to publish it.

To especially Shelly and Vijay, Kim and Roby Chandhok I am extremely thankful for preparing the first draft electronically along with helpful suggestions. The various discussions, with Rekha Jhanji, A.R. Khan, Vijay Bhardwaj, Sukrita Paul Kumar, Mohan Agarwal, Kishwar Shirali, Irene Winters, Goutam Biswas, Kapila Vatsyayan, Sehdev Kumar and Sharat Kumar, helped greatly to clarify my thoughts. To all of them and other colleagues, I am indebted.

To Keshav Malik, who very carefully edited the manuscript with many serious corrections, I am beholden, along with his wife Usha who has given much support as always.

Mrs P. Vijaylaxmi Rao unstintly typed the manuscript many times over; to her I am much obliged.

It is to Mr Shakti Malik of Abhinav Publications who decided to publish this book that many thanks are genuinely due.

The forbearance, equanimity and patience of my mother Annaji always sustained me in my modest efforts; to her I am grateful.

Finally, it was Anjali who empowered me to complete this monograph; to her I express my deep appreciation.

New Delhi
August 1988

S.C. Malik

List of Figures

1

Introduction

Evolutionary Perspectives

THE cosmos, as one knows, is a system which comprises thousands of millions of galaxies, each galaxy in turn being made up of thousands of millions of stars and their satellites in different evolutionary stages. The light which one sees raying from these stars and galaxies is often fossil light or light of those celestial bodies that may no longer exist. Towards the outer rim of one of these galaxies — the Milky Way — is a star of only medium size, and of moderate temperature, already yellowing into old age, the sun. One of the several cosmic fragments circling the sun is our planet earth, and living on its very thin crust are we, and our fellow companions — the animals and plants. The earth's core is simmering with intense heat. In other words life is so precarious that even a slight fractional change in temperature, or in the gravitational field, etc. will snuff it out at once.

The earth is at least ten thousand million years old, while the earliest forms of life appeared some three thousand million years ago, though today we can only reconstruct one-third of this evolution. Both organic and inorganic evolutions indicate similar developmental processes, of which the themes of diversity and unity are characteristic. Diversity is very obviously exemplified by the two million or more different varieties of organisms that are living today and the many more that existed in the past. But the basic unity of fundamental life process — from viruses to man — is not as obvious, since it is expressed by such processes as autosynthesis, reproduction and adaptation. Moreover, one of the achievements of twentieth-century science has been to show that living systems are the consequences of an extremely complex organization of non-living material which continues to operate in accordance with the same physio-chemical principles in organic material. For example, the composition of genetic material is a good illustration of this coordination of physio-chemical processes that control living organisms; it is the infinitesimal biochemical structural features which control organic life. Thus, today, we know that man, life and the earth are part and parcel of the same systems of energy and matter which are spread out sparsely in the vast universe, in the form of planets, stars and galaxies that travel around like excited molecules and atoms in many ways reflecting the microcosm.

In the long history of the earth, man just appeared about a little over a million years ago, he of course belongs to a group of mammals known as the Primates and in which are included monkeys and apes. The direction of human evolution has exhibited the same pattern of divergent evolution and extinction which holds true for other animals. But the commonness is not merely in terms of biology, since such aspects as sociability, hierarchy and territoriality also exist in non-human primates; features of social groupings which until recently were thought to belong exclusively to man. Nevertheless, man is not merely a biological creature. The shift from the earliest ape-man, at least 2-3 million years ago, to modern man, in the short period of a million years amply testifies to the selective advantages gained because of trends in the area of culture (Washburn 1961).

The main feature which makes man unique in the animal kingdom is the attribute of culture, even though cultural evolution is a reflection of our biotic characteristics. This, since without large brains and free hands our cultural inheritance would be lost. According to one view culture should not be considered anything more unique for man than are the characteristics which we attribute to various other animals; for example, if we ask questions about the thick hide of the hippopotamus, these questions are just as pertinent as the ones which we ask about man and his culture. Nevertheless, cultural evolution is non-biological in the sense that it is inherited by large members of a society independently of genetic origins, and each generation is able to preserve and pass on to each succeeding generation the accumulated information. It is well known that the social inheritance of acquired knowledge proceeds at a rapid rate, actually independent of micro-evolutionary changes in human populations. Of course, the maximum phases of this accelerated sociocultural evolution began only during the last 5,000 years, or about 5 per cent of human evolution. At any rate, without getting into the debate of whether man is all nature or all culture and history, we may state that man is both the product of nature as well as nurture, and that the organic or the biological and the superorganic or the cultural dimensions of man and his evolution are mutually interrelated and are not exclusive or independent of each other (Dobzhansky 1962).

Today, this biological and cumulative cultural inheritance has resulted in man's recent domination of the earth due to his technical and scientific mastery of the environment. Of course, it has also resulted into an overpopulated mankind, which at the same time has increased its capacity to "overkill" fellow beings. The reasons can obviously be deduced from human history and evolution; that not only *Homo sapiens* enter a new phase when culture evoluted but it also equipped the over-made-ape with more than survival; he became not only the sole tool-making animal but also a social, economic, political and ethical animal. It is for these reasons, we might recall, that many magnificent civilizations, cultures and societies have disappeared in the past; one of the causes most likely being that rigidity prevented mental development to keep pace with technological advances or, as suggested by others, civilizations have a pattern of evolution and extinction similar to the processes of biology. In any case, having produced "cultured" man, evolution entered a strange new phase specially because of the development of consciousness and self-awareness, the adaptive significance of which has been aptly put forth by Hallowel (1960):

> The attribute of self-awareness, which involves man's capacity to discriminate himself as an object in a world of objects other than himself, is as central to our understanding of the prerequisites of man's social and cultural mode of adjustments as it is for the psychodynamics of the individual. A human social order implies a mode of existence that has meaning for the individual at the level of self-awareness. A human social order, for example, is always a moral order. ... It is man's capacity for and development of self-awareness that makes such unconscious psychological mechanisms as repression, rationalization, and so on of adaptive importance for the individual. ... Man, unlike his animal kin, acts in a universe that he has discovered and made intelligible to himself as an organism not only capable of consciousness but also of self-consciousness and reflective thought. ... An organized social life in man, since it transcends purely biological and geographical determinants, cannot function apart from communally recognized meanings and values, or apart from the psychological structuralization of individuals who make these their own.

However, man's capacity for self-awareness and self-reflection, if it has brought forth many awesome gifts, has also given him a dreadfully heavy load of responsibilities. Self-knowledge and self-awareness have been the causes of a tragic discord in the soul of man ever since he was able to distinguish between what was, what is and what ought to be, even though it is this consciousness which allows him also to take decisions.

At any rate, today, the critical stage has been reached when mankind's decision alone will decide its destiny, for we are acutely aware that unless we learn to control population expansion, nuclear weapons, the polluted environment, etc. we are likely to be extinct. Moreover, the adaptive solution for survival lies in a psychic or mental development which lags far behind mankind's scientific and technological advances. Thus modern man's quest in the twentieth century is really to give a meaning and pattern to life individually as well as collectively in order to avoid a sense of alienation: he has to re-establish the relationship with reality in terms of scientific knowledge. For example, the latter presents a notion of infinity in the universe of neither a beginning nor an end; these notions of infinity leave man in a vacuum so that he has a need to reconcile the idea of infinity with such a finite time as his lifespan.

In another sense, the problem of alienation also arises among academics such as anthropologists, archaeologists and historians because in making temporal and spatial cross-cultural comparisons we become observers and spectators of not only others but even of our own culture and society. It is in this process of self-enlightenment that each of us is often freed from the limitations of his own cultural environment and in this reorientation process the problem of alienation also arises (Manners and Kaplan 1969). In the industrialized nations, this increased awareness has caused a dilemma which perhaps is due to, according to Marxian theorists, the social and economic contradictions that are inherent in a capitalistic or a semi-socialistic society. But the responsibility for disharmony and discontent among younger individuals is due also to the rapid social, economic and political changes which have made traditional values and moral absolutes inadequate for providing answers to questions about human existence that confront modern man. Moreover, computer efficiency, the production–consumption syndrome, time-and-motion study, the inevitability of progress and myriads of impersonal and inhuman relationships which are characteristic of large organizations; all these developments have failed to satisfy the youth who are very sensitively conscious of the inadequacies of mere materialism and "progress". It is therefore important that attempts be made to reflect on re-establishing man's relationship with the external world, by a re-evaluation of the meaning of life in an age of specialization when knowledge has become divorced from synthesis, thought and speculation. But the need of the modem world is not to revert to traditional answers, it is to freshly grope for the meaning of existence in our own terms, for this age and day with an eye on tomorrow, albeit the old answers cannot be ignored.

It is agains this brief but broad canvas that the implications of the philosophy of evolution and its various problems and paradoxes are outlined below.

1. It has been stated above that in man has arisen not only the capacity for culture but also an awareness that unravels the laws of nature. But it is in the extreme form of this thinking that there has been once again a self-glorification of man since some believe that it is with him that the cosmos entered a new eon; that he alone is endowed with awareness. But since man has a biological ancestry, should not some characteristics of incipient awareness also be present in his animal antecedents? In addition, in terms of probability and the knowledge about the infinitesimal microscopic size of the earth in the universe, is it really possible that he alone is endowed with these faculties and no one else, anywhere in the universe? Chances are that there must be life, similar or different, but equal, if not better, elsewhere in the universe. But in case we persist in believing that man is unique in a vast cosmos, then the problem of his existence or of his survival and extinction would not matter, for the unique exists on its own and for itself, unless we believe in the theory of special creation, but then we cannot lend credence to human evolution. Furthermore, even if we are unique, progress need not be inevitable, and to consider human evolution as the zenith or the end product has also no cogent reasoning behind it. What is more, in terms of evolution, there is no reason why man should not retrogress and head towards extinction like all the other species which have disappeared earlier. Thus, from the long evolutionary point of view man may be both on the verge of a magnificent era or he may be equally on the verge of extinction, destroying with him a minute cosmic fragment — the earth.
2. We are fairly certain that man is part of both inorganic and organic evolution, being governed similarly by its various norms, laws and patterns. But it appears somewhat inexplicable that out of a general biological phenomenon has arisen the superorganic which makes man lay claim to his autonomy and even to his own self-determination.

In other words, a by and large causal evolutionary process has given rise to a species which is considered by itself to be free and, therefore, indeterminate in a sense. Of course, evolution is not deterministic because random choice, chance variations, etc. are conditions of biological evolution. This indeterminateness may also be justified by stating that modern quantum physics recognizes indeterminateness and probability as ultimate attributes of nature, and today's physics describes the potentialities of nature rather than any determinate laws. But while these indeterminate conditions do exist in nature, in the case of man it is he who himself has to self-consciously choose and decide; and today, the exercise of this choice cannot any longer be a random one for the stakes are too high. Moreover, we must remember that chance, probability and indeterminateness are not identical or synonymous with man's freedom of choice and his volition. Nevertheless, these theoretical developments in the physical and natural world may make human freedom and indeterminateness justifiable and intelligible. Hence, we might state that since indeterminacy and probability are attributes of both the inorganic and organic worlds, their appearance in man should cause no surprise: albeit the argument is not quite so convincing.

3. We know that in biological evolution a characteristic feature of survival is the need for the self-preservation of the species. In man, it is his capacity for culture which has helped him survive and progress. But man is not only capable of self-determination and preservation in accordance with his biological attributes, he is also capable of total self-negation, of a denial of freedom for himself and even capable of suicide not only individually but also collectively. As stated earlier, he is more than a tool-making animal. However, in the context of today, he has no choice but to direct his own evolution through a self-conscious effort by means of his own wits. In biological terms, this would be part of the need for survival and self-preservation, though it is not instinct but freedom and right choice of action which will decide

his future, through wisdom and by a positive re-evaluation of his values. Ironically, he has no other choice, the other alternative being one of destroying himself. It thus means that the freedom of choice in terms of his survival is limited and, in a broad sense, his direction is "determined", that is, if he wants to continue to preserve his species.

4. When we speak of human freedom, this is really an idealized situation because each man's potentialities are really limited. For instance, in the total life pattern of each individual there are three themes which govern his behaviour, viz. (i) body centred, (ii) psyche-centred and (iii) culture-centred. The chief variables under each of these themes are, respectively, (i) biological metabolism, life cycle, health, disease, sex and procreation; (ii) emotions, social orientation, environment, dominance and (iii) language, knowledge, religions, arts, ethos, etc. (Washburn 1961). Therefore, human freedom in terms of cultural evolution is relative, and even the freedom which is available and possible, say to the adherents of a culture, is existent to the extent that they conform to the cultural norms and traditional institutions and it is in this sense alone that they feel free, even if this for the most part is because of the unawareness of not being free, or being under any constraints. Consequently, if the above themes are undeniable in acting as constraints in individual or group behaviour, what then is the true position of human freedom and how is this to be expressed and achieved? Is man really free? One form of freedom for the anthropologist and others, as stated above, is due to a greater awareness of and freedom from one's own culture. But this freedom from one's own culture often further enhances the dilemma and problem of alienation, of negation and of annihilation, even though one may be able to justify this rootlessness by an indeterminate metaphysics and a modern version of physical reality. Is freedom, then, only a state of mind of the individual who is culturally conditioned to believe so?

5. Thus, if human freedom is to be expressed only in terms of

the freedom of the self or the person, how is one to determine the nature of this free self? (Bidney 1980). It has been widely suggested that, when by virtue of self-reflection the mind treats itself as an object of knowledge, it is the beginning of the mind's power of self-determination and self-expression. Therefore, a knowledge of the mind and the self is the beginning of psychological and moral wisdom, and the quest of one's relationship with the external world is a part of this process. It is in this process that one discovers what one refers to as the will of a person, since this awareness is the only way whereby one is able to consciously choose from amongst the given alternatives. In terms of evolution, this self-awareness and self-realization might provide the answer to our problems today, because greater the number of individuals who are aware of making consciously chosen decisions, greater are the chances to positively direct human evolution and history. But the exercise of volition leads us to further complications.

6. We have man's will — and his freedom — resulted from the development of the mind and the self. But these attributes emerge as a consequence of the evolutionary process which is part of the pattern of the universe itself. Therefore, strangely enough, if it is the evolutionary process which is the cause of the will, can the will be self-determined? Because, in metaphysical terms, a free will has to be totally free if it is to exercise choice and, strictly speaking, it cannot have a cause for this implies a "conditioned" will. Consequently, if we admit that free will and human autonomy constitute crucial dimensions of human existence (because man is able to exercise his choice) therein itself lies another paradox. Is it possible that will and freedom emerge from and are subject to the determination of nature and culture at the same time? If this be true, how do we postulate a free will — as the action of man's mind — along with culture? Of course, as social scientists we might answer that the mind may only utilize culture within its limitations for creative achievement. But then, in the metaphysical sense, this would be an exercise

in choice which is relative to what can be done given the constraints, and not at all a "free" will.

7. On the other hand, if we do admit the postulate that man is endowed with a free will and freedom of choice, the sciences of culture and society become impossible since a free will implies an essential arbitrariness or causelessness in human affairs. Hence, this means the independence of man from nature. But can we possibly isolate man (a product of nature, as evolution shows), unless we attribute his origin to some supernatural causes? On the contrary, if we visualize the development of man, society, culture and his mind and will, etc. as equally subject to generalized processes and laws that are applicable to other objects of the cosmos, then must not man also be part of an overall pattern of the cosmos, perhaps fulfilling a function unknown to him? However, this argument has shades of some kind of determinism. Moreover, does it not counteract the statement made earlier that some form of indeterminateness is also a part of the evolution of the cosmos? Shall we ever know for certain?

The answers and solutions to the problems and paradoxes mentioned above can only be guesses tempered by some kind of faith or belief, even if this be in terms of a scientific and humanistic philosophy. We might mention here in passing that the other alternative within the theory of evolution is provided by the Omega Point referred to by Pierre Teilhard de Chardin (1959). For him, the direction of human evolution is towards a collective, harmonious superconsciousness by which the earth is being covered gradually, and this process will ultimately lead to a single unit of a new dimension of Thought, like the dimensions of Time and Space. This conception does provide us with a coherent theory which answers some of the questions about the direction and meaning of human existence. But like other theological and creational myths present in all religion, these answers are not demonstrable by any scientifically established process even though they do give man stronger hope and support in the ostensibly vast void of the cosmos than what any scientific and humanistic philosophy may provide.

The idea of man's place in the evolution of the universe is one of the cornerstones on which the thinking of modern man has been based, and this era was ushered in forcefully by the theory of evolution as enunciated by Darwin. Nevertheless, today, there is no philosophy or a total coherent-holistic world view which accounts for the dilemma of human existence, specially within the framework of the evolutionary theory. Man has yet to rediscover in the present century his place in this pattern of total cosmic evolution. This quest is crucial because the man of today knows that he no longer stands at the centre of the universe, as a special creation; that the universe is no longer presided over by an overlord who may be implored or propitiated and who cares for him. In fact, the theories of evolution, relativity and probability and so on make him acutely conscious that cosmic evolution is essentially aimless, having neither a beginning nor an end. Nevertheless, it is a strange paradox that despite this knowledge, man's technological and scientific control over the environment today has no parallel in human history. He has — on all evidence — entered into a new form of extreme egocentricity and anthropomorphism. In short, despite a denial of deity or any supernaturalness attributed to him in his evolution, he has once again begun to glorify himself (being a consequence perhaps of an extreme form of materialism) as a peculiar and unique phenomenon in the scheme of things. Today, we somehow seem to overlook the fact of our puny existence which the study of evolution impresses upon us; perhaps because this theory sees human development not only within the framework of non-human living and non-living nature but also within the totality of cosmic evolution. Thus, man's existence has somehow to be visualized in this total scheme — despite his ephemeral nature — because his uniqueness will only represent an aberration and a freak momentary existence on the cosmic scale. Of course, if man considers himself to be unique it may be just another expression of his common biological attribute, namely, that of survival and of self-preservation.

However, it should be clear that evolution does not guarantee the "progress" of man to be inevitable, or that it is vouchsafed by any law of nature. Of course, man has always striven for progress but it is only in terms of what he alone regards as his betterment at a given time and place. But even here there has been no uniformity of opinion as to what is "good" or what is not; for example, human nature for the optimist is good while for the pessimist it is bad, violent and rotten — and upon this depends "progress". Therefore, apart from the realization of the values which are important at a given time, and at a given place, for their own sake (existential truths), there are no universal criteria whereby one can ascertain any eternal truths — though now the common agreement may be in the view that mankind should survive. But how does it become possible in general to judge whether we have taken the right decision and selected the wisest of values? Today, whether it is in the context of saving mankind from destruction or of liberating two-thirds of mankind from social injustice and economic inequality, it is only the values of confirmation and affirmation through a self-conscious effort, through self-reflection and with the freedom for open development of newer ideas and values for all mankind which will help man "progress". In the evolutionary sense, man is a determinant of human behaviour and evolution. Consequently, he has to direct his own evolution — of entire mankind — through a deliberate well thought out choice and not be dragged along either by the philosophies of Fate, Supernaturalism, Nature or even by History. Today, history and evolution move forward by human consent alone, and it is only human decision which may act as the effective historical cause.

The dilemma nevertheless remains because the presence of choice, indeterminateness and probability as a factor in nature does not allow culture and historical reality to be reduced to any natural law or pattern; because as we have also stated that human consciousness is subject to its own freedom, to its own judgement and to its own choice. Of course, we may state that the designs and patterns which we see around us are, in fact, only heuristic devices made by man himself for his own understanding, that is if he seeks a pattern it is because this philosophy and metaphysics of an aimless and indeterminate cosmos in human affairs and in evolution is difficult to accept, because, in terms of the explanation of human existence it leads an individual nowhere. But if human

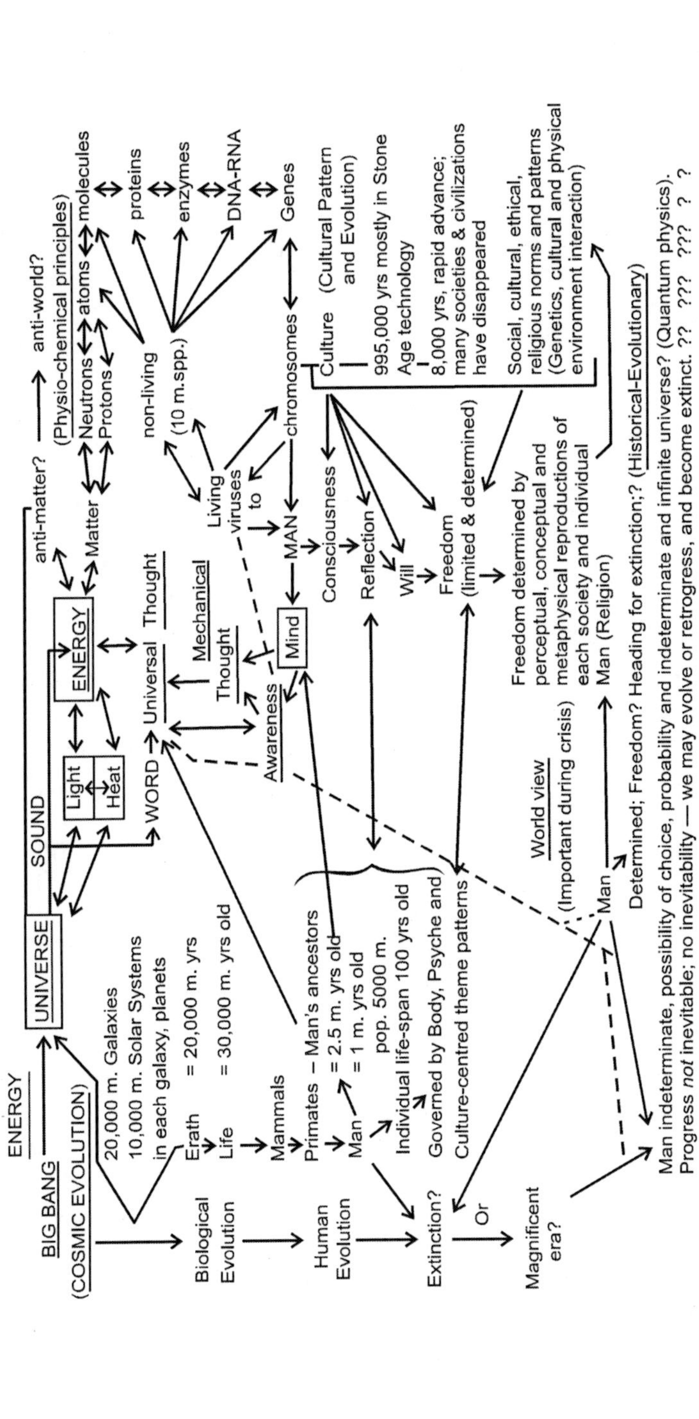

fig.1.1: Evolutionary background

Explanation to *fig.* 1.1

Graphically illustrates the complicated processes and variables involved in the current evolutionary theoretical accepted scenario. Some say Consciousness is a by-product of the physical or somatic developments, especially of the brain. This is the majority accepted view. For others it is all happening within Consciousness, an energy system and the apparent phenomenal or somatic world is a sub-system (primary, secondary and tertiary and of this vast Consciousness or Energy) system or Space itself which is without specific forms. Most of the forms are a projection of the mental makeup that is socio-culturally determined by a world view of different cultural groups both synchronically and diachronically. This is not to cover the way plant, animals and other creatures view the world, especially dependent on what sense organs are involved, which are determined by evolutionary processes. This is how Homo sapiens has come in existence, determined vertically and horizontally by all that has gone before and at present. In other words, humankind is interlinked to all else, it is not an isolated and only human-centred universe. Today however, humankind has become extremely self-centred, and so much so that in this narcissistic obsession it is killing its own kind by the millions, not to speak of all other creatures. Until now no other species has behaved in this manner. This is also reflects a disorder in the psyche which is of a very serious nature, not only humankind is heading towards extinction but with it the entire natural world, if not the planet itself. The urgent need, unless its too late, is to be aware of all this, to contemplate on this grim scenario, which is a special characteristic of man, or so we believe. We ourselves name ourselves Man the Wise, Homo sapiens!.

Thus the direction for this serious dilemma is to examine this human set up namely, the nature of the little self, nature of thought, consciousness, the psycho-somatic structure, the importance of language. In short, who am I? It is to relook into basic pre-suppositions, assumptions, the fundamental philosophic foundations which need a serious re-examination. As Socrates has said, "An unexamined life is not worth living" For example, in whatever manner it has come to be widely prevalent this is the Cartesian statement "I think therefore I am" is running most of our lives. In this statement which is a linguistic one, neither the nature of "I" nor thinking is looked into, and mostly of all "I am". It is possible to state inversely that "I am therefore there is thinking" or thinking, eating, walking, all actions are possible because of I AM, this existence is the basic foundation. Furthermore, then I is without questioning presumed to be the body, this body which is the somatic structure pointed out as "body", a linguistic statement with further qualifications, that the mental setup of a socio-cultural "I" or "me" is based on this statement again unqualified when one says, "My Body".

It is further unquestioned that this name and form refer to a "me" or "I" has come about without one's volition, namely, the body (this body) came into existence on its own in one sense, in another that it is the product of long evolutionary history. Genealogical genetic ancestry which is further limited to not only the solar system, it is part of not only it but the entire milky-way galaxy, and then from there the entire universe. You or I is normally conditioned to believe as separate selves, especially in the modern world, little realizing that we are linked and interrelated to all else socio-culturally, linguistically and physically also to plants animals, the elements, the latter being a product of planet earth which in turn is link and interrelated to all the planetary and galaxial systems.

nature and culture could not have been pre-determined, then, can man himself really predetermine or determine — be a cause — of his own future? Is this not a form of ethnocentricity? Moreover, armed with this same knowledge of self-sufficiency can man — finite — really establish a relationship with an indeterminate, vast and infinite universe? This manner of thought — of neither a beginning nor an end in which human existence is reduced to relatively "nothing" both in space and time — can lead to some very exasperating situations, at least for the individual who is left in a vacuum (so to speak) in an aimless and indeterminate universe; knowing fully well that this is what it is really like. Here, it may help us somewhat if we realize that this dilemma is intrinsic in a situation when there is freedom of choice available and in which decision-making is involved, that is, an element of unpredictability and indeterminacy has to be present because, otherwise, the problem of choice would not be available if we instinctively knew — without awareness — as to what we want to do. In any case, in historical and evolutionary sense, today, man has to decide between the various possibilities and, therefore, the choice remains with him while inevitability, predetermination and resignation cannot be a basis of twentieth-century philosophy.

The theory of evolution, change and progress does not claim to offer any total philosophy as such or any directions that may take; it only explains to us certain aspects of his emergence and his background. It cannot and does not pretend to give any total explanations of man and culture, though it does provide a backdrop for a world view and a way of life (Malik 1972) (*fig*. 1.1).

2

Obsolescence in Research
The Biological Analogy

MODERN science and technology originated in a specific historical–philosophical climate of western Europe; and of course there are certain fundamental philosophical presuppositions behind these developments. They may be summarized as follows:

The Universe

1. It is mechanical, with no intentionality or purpose. Even though it may be dynamic, it is a huge machine and not an organism of consciousness. In being so, it is indifferent to man, and so it needs to be mastered.
2. The universe is real to the extent that it can be externalized, quantified, measured in terms of mass, dimensions, colour, taste and so on, though these characteristics are not ultimately real.
3. The internal nature of man is subjective and other than the external — and which alone can be objective and true.
4. Matter precedes intelligence — the latter must be explained in terms of the former which may be inert though subject to aimless forces.
5. Time is linear, sequential; and space essentially uniform. Energy is basically the same, not gross nor subtle; it may be more or less quantitative. Time, space and energy are only

external, i.e. real, and are independent of the level of the perceiving consciousness.

6. Importance is given to the causal notion, in terms of complexity and intelligence.

Man

1. Essentially a rational cognizer; body with a mind localized in it, an "engine with a will", an atomic being, individual without any transpersonal spirit.
2. There is no essential hierarchy of a being or consciousness among men, or within man; even if this were so, it would be irrelevant to knowledge and the organization of society, governments, etc.
3. Man, as he is, is a imperfect being, and yet the measure of all things.

Knowledge-Truth

1. Knowledge is an end in itself, except perhaps for the betterment of the estate of man.
2. There is one truth—if it was Christianity once, it is science now.
3. Subject and object can be completely separated, i.e. without a need for an earlier study of one's self.
4. Reason is the only faculty by which knowledge may be obtained; even experiments are extensions of this faculty. But sensations and feelings are not true perceptions.
5. True knowledge is obtained by proceeding from the part to the whole.
6. Importance is bestowed on detaching one's self from the object of study, rather by participation and experiencing the object of study.
7. Reality is a mental construct; knowledge is abstract and general, not a vision or experience of particulars.
8. True knowledge is quantitative, not qualitative—what can be quantified is independent of place and function.

9. True knowledge leads to predictions of what is known, since it is based on external, repeatable perceptions; only that which is externalized is available to true knowledge.
10. The truth and falsity of propositions is self-evident, irrespective of the person who says it.
11. As knowledge has nothing to do with beingness or consciousness, it is not esoteric, i.e. it requires no extra-normal preparation to be discovered or to be understood.
12. In principle, in the making of actual observations (and not in the interpretation of data), the observer can always be replaced by scientific instruments.
13. The dichotomy of faith–knowledge — perhaps is more a consequence of the Scientific Revolution rather than a presupposition: that truth and knowledge reside in dimensions other than from those in which there are religious considerations.

What has been summarized above is well known. However, despite new directions of knowledge and higher research in general, the implementation of policies at the applied level continues to be governed by obsolete presuppositions. To recapitulate some of the premises for example, that continue to shape current thinking, these are: (i) Cartesian dualism which separates mind from matter; (ii) metaphors, which have their context in physicalisms, are used in describing and explaining mental phenomena, e.g. power, tension, energy, and social forces; and (iii) certain antiaesthetic assumptions that are derived from physical sciences, which state that all phenomena (including the mental) shall be studied and evaluated only in quantitative terms. The epistemological implications, and the corollaries of such notions, have further generated the following developments in pragmatic terms:

i. The "struggle for survival" mentality which has accentuated monstrous overgrowth, wars, tyranny and pollution. The stark demonstration of the practical results of these premises has not yet revealed their patent falseness to most academics, intellectuals and policymakers.

ii. Intellectually, while these current alternatives are available such as systems theory, cybernetics, holistic medicine, ecology and gestalt psychology, whose premises are "revolutionary", we continue to ignore these better ways of understanding the world (Dossey 1982).

iii. By ignoring the aesthetic values and vision of poets and mystics, these assumptions have even misled people away from the true foundations of religion.

iv. The effects of this "unthought way of life" have split human civilization wide open. Even at the level of economics, the emphasis continues to be one about "taking sides" with either the capitalists or the communists. It is as if there were no other choice except to be torn between these two extremes of anti-intellectual, anti-mystic, anti-poetic, or else anti-rational and anti-scientific fanaticism.

v. Also, at the level of understanding religious systems the same division between the sacred and the secular is being promoted alongside many other exaggerations. So much so are the results of this that various "religious" movements have arisen in the West, even if some of these had their origin in the East (Bateson 1979).

Almost all modern institutions, and especially research institutions, even at the expense of trying to avoid the swamps of all sorts of extremism, continue to pay attention to the above-mentioned obsolete notions. They have, of course, tried (or pretended) to maintain standards of excellence (Malik 1971b). But is it possible to do so, in the face of the general overgrowth of distrust, vulgarity, exploitation of resources, victimization of persons and quick commercialism? In short, within a framework of greed, frustration, fear and hatred, is it really expected of these centres to produce a new vision of society? Unfortunately, such obsolete notions even govern research in technical schools where people are taught to be engineers, doctors and lawyers; the basic philosophy here also is one which leads to "success" in "trade", that is, it is the same old dualistic pragmatism. Within this framework of obsolescence, it once again amounts to emptiness

— or mere motions in the air, a pretence of doing, of producing results.

The question is not debatable even in the context of the "older" or "younger" generation, for all of us function within the earlier framework of reference. Even if the younger generation tries to put up a pretence of revolution, the young too soon become the establishment. It is as if this philosophy of an "either/or" framework has overtaken every sphere of life. Even as it concerns process of thought it is a choice between rigour or imagination. But to emphasize either of these, without a balancing, is the reason for a great deal of confusion and chaos. The situation now borders on insanity for society as a whole impinges as it does on every walk of life.

At every level, there is a struggle for power; shall we say it is only a mental one now, which at one time had a physical dimension. The struggle is now in the context of social power (including politico-economic areas), no longer is there struggle for such values as honour, beauty or even truth. While everybody seems to talk of "something being wrong" with culture, particularly the one of the educational system, the diagnosis and its solution have been misdirected. For example, one solution suggested is that if students were adequately represented on the governing bodies of their institutions, matter will improve, that is by the very fact of taking part in power groups. But it is clear that such battles for power neither bring about any significant change nor leave aside a better system of a totally transformed educational process. No amount of new structures, equipment and rearrangement of status or power groups will make any difference as long as obsolete notions continue to dominate or create non-issues over which the battle continues to take place time and again.

The immediate need is for a rethinking about the very premises which govern modern institutions. It is only with a recognition of underlying reality on which we tread, that the second step of solutions will naturally come about. This awakening itself will provide us insight on how to act effectively, appropriately. Many people think that delving into this kind of philosophical foundation is not practicable. But all the so-called practical (misplaced notion of concreteness) attempts to improve and reform society — and its educational systems — are not workable. A return to a re-examination of the fundamental philosophical propositions, or the essence, alone may transform society. This is the one, practical down-to-earth approach and this is what is likely to correct the basic flaws. But most policymakers, bureaucrats, and those who are on the governing bodies of research institutions do not even consider it fit to discuss conceptual and theoretical issues even though such perceptions have a significant place in the development of society. In the absence of such discussions, obsolete and unthought of premises become the source of anti-intellectual preferences, using the word "intellectual" in the sense of a search for truth. There is clearly an imbalance somewhere.

The problem of obsolescence, or one-sided progress, is not one of being static. It implies that there are some parts of the system, which compared with the obsolete ones, are moving ahead, while more of the others are lagging or left behind. In a static system there would be no obsolescence, since there would be a balancing of various parts. In terms of understanding such processes, there also exist two components in biological evolution, just as there seems to be a similar double structure in the mental process. The biological process may be used as a paradigm for understanding current notions of thought, cultural change and education (Bateson 1979).

The evolutionary processes — biologically speaking — imply the notion of survival, which means the maintenance of a steady state through successive generations. In negative terms, it usually tends to take shape in its extreme dimensions — meaning the avoidance of the death of the largest system. Similarly, when this survival notion becomes a mere ideational one — mental creation unrelated to biology, i.e. the survival of the idea, or idea of the system, without taking into account the environment or ecology — then it indeed becomes very destructive since the survival of the system cannot be larger than the ecological conditions. Survival — historically speaking — depends upon two contrasting phenomena or processes whereby adaptive action may be achieved. Evolution has to move in two directions: (1) the inward development of regularity and physiology of the living creature; and (2) outwardly towards vagaries and demands of the environment. But these contrasting components somehow seem interestingly to move in two contrary directions. Biologically the inner development — the embryology or the "epigenesis" — is conservative and demands that every new thing shall conform or be compatible with the regularities of the earlier status quo. In natural selection, thinking of new features of anatomy or physiology, it is transparent that one side of the selection process favours those new items which will not upset the old system. This is the minimum necessary conservatism required.

In contrast, the outside world is perpetually changing in order as to receive creatures which have undergone changes, almost insisting upon change. The animal or plant can never be readymade! While the internal insists upon compatibility it is never sufficient for the development in the life of the organism. The creature itself must achieve a change of its own body, clearing certain somatic characteristics by use, habit, hardship and nurture. But these acquired characteristics cannot become hereditary or be directly incorporated into the deoxyribonucleic acid (DNA). In cultural or organizational terms this allows creatures to transmit certain adaptive features through channels other than the genetic one. Of course, it is the genetic material which allows for this kind of an adaptability via natural external selection, say, of those offsprings who happen (due to the random shuffling of genes or random creation) to have a greater propensity for developing certain survival features that allow it to function under changing external conditions. While the individual body undergoes adaptive changes under external pressure, natural selection acts upon the gene pool of the population. It is an acquired characteristic which sets the context for the selection of genetic changes that are necessary for coping under the stress situation of the population at large. It is these newly acquired habits which stay in a condition for natural selection. But this does not make them any less important if these are not carried on, i.e. passed on by the DNA.

It is interesting to note that the same principle applies conversely to the acquisition of bad habits at a social level. This is what surely sets the context for the selection of ultimately lethal genetic propensities. For instance, it is clear from the way civilization is heading towards its total destruction, i.e. it is getting set within this kind of genetic depression or entropy. In this case the same principle is applicable to mental and cultural processes, since their context is logically within the total framework of biological evolution. Man dominates the planet and through mental processes is directing his, and even the earth's, biological dimensions. It is the internal selection in biology which always stresses compatibility with the immediate past, and over long evolutionary time it is the internal selection which determines the homologies. Internal selection is conservative and this conservatism shows itself most strongly in embryology and the preservation of abstract form. In a word, conservatism in such a way is rooted in coherence and compatibility, and it is in this that there is also involved rigour in the mental process. This is where the roots of obsolescence may be looked for.

There is an inbuilt fear that in the very fact of looking into fundamental suppositions we might lose coherence, clarity, compatibility and even sanity, that is, if we let go of the old or the "obsolete". But obsolescence has a reference to the contrast between two components; i.e. if in a cultural system one part lags behind then we know that another part must have evolved too fast. In terms of natural processes as seen in the analogy of biological evolution, that the one root of the very rapid movement of human civilization is to be found in the process of exclusive external selection. Consequently, in the growth of our civilization imbalance is quite transparent even if the deep roots of the problem are only truly clear to a very few. Something is out of step in the steering of these two components, i.e. the movement without and the movement within. Thus rapid progress may be seen on the one hand, in the external technological developments and progress; in this we may include thought which at the superficial level may also be considered a technology and matter. On the other hand, there is the lagging behind of the inner psychological and psychic developments. There is thus an imbalance, or of being psychologically not in tune with the enormous external adaptations and control, or exploitation of the environment.

At another level one may say that "imagination", once again in the context of concepts or "survival" notions, has gone too far ahead of rigour (as deep thinking of basics). Thus, it, development/ progress, seems like a nightmare since the dream is not being corrected by any internal rigour or even external reality. To speak even from the viewpoint of social reality the laws applicable today have not caught up with technological development and the fast pace of dimensions of research in science. In other words, the old ways of thought lag behind new advances all around.

These developments of the day — of abstract dualistic relationships and which are necessary components in the varied processes of change — seem to have occurred under many familiar labels, e.g. pattern/quantity, form/function, letter/spirit, rigour/ imagination, homology/analogy, calibration/feedback and so on. Individuals may favour one or the other components of this dualism and they will then be labelled as conservatives/radicals or liberals and so on. And these labels, which divide and define the poles of contrast in terms of dialectical necessities of the living world, are indications of certain deeper epistemological truths (Bateson 1979).

However, while it is obvious that there cannot be day without night nor form without function, such divisions are somehow placed in opposition to each other, rather than as compliments a question really of how an appropriate or practical combination may be achieved. This kind of complimentarity does indeed occur in most of the Asian, at least Chinese and Indian world views, where these contrasting abstractions are interlinked within the totality, or whole. Or, even apart from the nascent Cartesian dualism in Christianity, the viewpoint of St. Thomas Acquinas indicates this totality and oneness almost like the Vedāntic tradition does. However, that wider viewpoint has somehow been lost due to narrowing obsession with technological materialism during the last some centuries.

It is perhaps easier to play with one half of the kind of adversarial game we have set up; and not easy to create a balance since that burdens us with the duty of rising above partisanship, or of not combining with any particular fad at both the research and policymaking levels. But at the social and cultural levels, there are no "equipment" barriers such as is the case with biological systems which prohibit adaptive features from becoming inheritable precisely in order to protect the gene system from too rapid change under possibly adverse environmental demands. Of course, the gene pool of the population is subject to change under natural selection; a clear recognition of differences, especially in biology, to achieve a more adaptive functioning. Yet the immediate individual bodily effects of functioning are never allowed to impinge the form, or individual genetic coding.

Thus, how is one to safely bring about changes as well as avoid obsolescence in functioning in order that descriptions of change may be summarized and coded, though not too fast, into the core of form? What happens in university systems, or other institutions, is that innovations become irreversibly adapted into the on-going system without being tested for long-time viability. But necessary changes are naturally resisted by the core of conservative individuals, who are the ones to resist "giving up" outdated notions and adaptations. Individual comfort or discomfort becomes the only criterion for a choice of social change. The basic contrast of logical typing between the member and the category is forgotten until discomforts are inexorably spawned by the new state of affairs.

Obsolescence cannot be avoided by simply speeding up change in a structure nor can it be avoided by simply slowing down functional changes. Clearly neither an overall conservatism nor an overall eagerness for change is appropriate. However, not seeing these two poles as necessary adversaries or opposites and combining them, may perhaps seem better than being merely partisan towards one of them alone. The way is to see, that henceforth these are not treated in the context of either/ or adversaries, i.e. as adversarial systems. The absence of an integrated approach straight leads to the irrelevant strength of one or the other, one of them tending to rule decision, without the balanced matching strength of the complete argument. Thus, it is not so much "power" as such that corrupts as its myth, it being equated with "energy", "tension" and the rest of those oft-used quasi-physical metaphors. These must be distrusted since, mythical abstractions — however much they be coveted — are seldom satiated (Bateson 1979).

The fact is that it is difficult for an adversary to see further than the dichotomy in which winning and losing in a combat of "survival" seems to be the only dimension of existence. This game like any game tempts one to make a "quick victory" by some covert moves rather than look for the best, the most sophisticated move, but which are hard to attain and maintain. Few people (and even less so those in the educational system) seem to have an eye on the longer view or gestalt. The need in the context of the crisis that civilization faces today, is to have a transformed, wider perspective, and which is what perspectives are about, to begin with, i.e. the very way of knowing how we know or see, in the context of true knowledge. This will allow our entire biocultural system to return to, or once again take recourse to, an appropriate synchrony or harmony of not only human civilization as a whole, but also within the total scheme of evolutionary movement.

3

New Ideas in Biology

Morphogenetic Fields, Evolution and Consciousness

PLANT physiologist Rupert Sheldrake (1983) has come up with some fundamental concepts about nature and consciousness that have far-reaching implications. This is the hypothesis of formative causation which postulates that the universe functions not so much by immutable loss as by habits or patterns created by the repetition of events several times. It is not only that all systems are regulated by known energy and material factors but also by invisible organizing fields. In this, fields of morphogenetic nature have no energy but are nevertheless causative because they serve as blueprints for form and behaviour. Suggesting thereby that whenever one member of species learns a new behaviour, the causative field for the species is changed ever so slightly. But if the behaviour is repeated for long enough, its "morphic resonance" affects the entire species. The invisible matrix is "morphogenetic field" derived from the word morphe, meaning form, and genesis, meaning come-into-being. For convenience the term is the "M-fields". Whenever an atom, a molecule, cell, organism or other "morphic unit" first comes into being it generates the M-field that regulates all subsequent units of the same type. The influence of the M-field involves action at a distance in both space and time rather than form being determined by physical loss outside time, i.e. it depends on morphic resonance across time. This kind of thinking moves into unchartered territory which would be unexplainable within the simple mechanistic hypothesis.

Experiments on rats, which carry out tasks that have been never done before, show that rats everywhere else suddenly start to do the same thing though removed at great distance. Not only that, we already know of certain skills that are learnt by rats of the next generation. This phenomenon discovered in the 1920s has not been explained unless it is seen within the hypothesis of morphic resonance. The concept of morphogenetic field has been in existence in embryology and developmental biology for eighty years in order to explain the problem not accounted for by genetic theory, that is how organisms inherit and maintain their specific structures. This hypothesis of "formative causation" involves a radical departure from the currently orthodox ways of looking at the world within the existing scientific structure. It certainly spells revolutionary implications for human existence.

Morphic Resonance: Some Examples

The idea of morphic resonance in the M-fields as the potential information for transmission of heritability is quite other than the genetic model. It has been simply explained by Sheldrake initially in terms of an analogy, which one commonly uses in any discussion on consciousness. This, in order that the large scientific and lay populations familiar with existing models may gain some ability to understand a totally different perspective which at first appears very jarring. This extremely unfamiliar context may be understood by imagining a person who is very intelligent and curious, such as a member of a tribal society cut-off from modern technological civilization, who knows nothing about electricity or electromagnetic radiation. Whether he is shown a radio or a television set for the first time, it will be very puzzling for him to hear or see voices or images on the screen. These might at first appear to him as "real", though once he looks inside the instrument there are only wires, condensers and other components. He might evolve a sophisticated hypothesis of these images in terms of complicated interactions between the various components of the set. The hypothesis may be considered very real if the images become distorted, or disappeared, when some of the components were removed. He would reject any notion at this point if someone suggested that the images appear from some very far distant sources that projected the images and voices from a main operating centre. He would reject this hypothesis as being very mystical or obscurantist in nature.

We know today that there are such radiations as X-ray, infrared and many others that are invisible to our gross sensory perceptions, yet which sophisticated instruments record and reproduce. But outside laboratory conditions, in everyday life, we have little notions on how many such invisible vibrations effect most of us not only from nature but even what has been called the aura — psychic vibrations — that surrounds each one of us, and the latter continuously changes its form as the thoughts and feelings of persons keep changing. It is sometimes for this reason that when two people interact and are physically near or distant to each other that there is a natural response of affinity or repulsion; this level also depending upon whether the aura coincides with harmony or discord.

At any rate, current thinking is based on quantification so that if, for this imaginary person, the set were switched off and the images disappeared he would be reinforcing his framework of a linear mind hypothesis, because he will note that the set does not differ in its weight when it is on, and when switched off. This viewpoint resembles the conventional approach to reality. But the hypothesis of formative causation does not involve a denial of the importance of the wires, transistors, etc. that correspond to DNA, protons, molecules. It however recognizes, in addition, the role or influence transmitted from outside the system; "transmitters" being past organisms of the same species. Those genetic changes can effect the inheritance of form or instinct by altering the tuning or by introducing distortions into the reception. But genetic factors do not fully account for the inheritance of form and instinct any more when the particular pictures on the screen of a television set can be explained in terms of the wiring-diagram alone.

Lyall Watson (1980) describes what is called "Hundredth monkey phenomenon" where the concept of morphic resonance is aptly applicable or relevant. Briefly, it may be recounted that Watson, who is a biologist, was working on a monkey tribe on an island near Japan where a new food, freshly dug sweet potatoes covered with sand and grit, was introduced. The monkeys obviously did not eat these dirty potatoes as opposed to the natural clean food they were otherwise comfortable in eating. Then, one eighteen-month old female somehow carried the potatoes to the stream and washed them before eating. This behaviour introduced a kind of cultural revolution for it involves abstraction, the identification of a concept, and a deliberate manipulation of several parameters in the environment. She taught her new behaviour to her mother and her playmates who in turn taught it to their mothers. Eventually many of the juvenile monkeys were doing the same thing who had come in contact with the children. Not only for those monkeys — who were taught directly — but practically the whole colony, moving through a kind of critical mass, was suddenly within the period (from learning this behaviour in the morning until the evening), easily following this pattern that was to become universal. Even more than on this island colony, in distant island colonies monkeys suddenly picked up the same behaviour. This is not unlike the well-known case of glycerine crystals still in jars, that begin to appear in other jars far away. Such biological behaviour suggests many other models or avenues available in evolution, other than those governed by "ordinary" natural selection. It is thus clear that this "hundredth monkey phenomenon" might account for ideas and fashions that spread through cultural patterns, i.e. when enough of us hold something to be true it becomes true for everyone.

The idea of invisible fields is not new as far as ancient philosophers are concerned, except that scientific hypotheses in the context of physics, chemistry and biology are finding it through different research methodologies and with identifiable data, and thereby contributing to the knowledge of consciousness. There is the notion of cosmic consciousness that is reflected in the individual consciousness using body and brain as vehicles and instruments for its own purpose, creation or self-realization. In the Upaniṣads several levels of gross, mental or subtle, causal and supra-causal and levels beyond, or even states beyond any levels, are well known. But these ideas bearing on physical phenomena are also mentioned by Plato who talks of ideal forms, as Aristotle of external forms, and many others of thought forms or layers of a mind of etherial substance in which all kinds of potentialities exist to materialize into the substance that is visible to us. Ergo, potentially everything already exists. Thus, just as there are magnetic fields, electrical fields, so also is biological data transmitted through similar regulatory field systems. Sheldrake has stated that M-fields are without mass or energy, challenging the assessment that energy is needed for a formulative field. This M-field is a blueprint that "causes" the creation of a form but contributes no energy as such.

Implications of Morphic Resonance

The notion of morphic resonance has implications at the sensory perception level such as in the dealing of physical sensations and especially in psychomotor skills, acupuncture, accelerated learning, behavioural conditioning, reinforcement, the apparent "body memory" of old traumas and so on. The hypothesis lends new credibility to such esoteric concepts as the memory of prior lifetimes, the resonant effect of group meditations to power, ritual, spiritual and the accumulative effect of an idea held by a number of individuals. This hypothesis is akin to what the physicist David Bohm's (1980) synthesis refers to, namely, the "enfolded" order, and the physical chemist Ilya Prigogine's (1985) proof of the ordering principle in entropy itself. The idea of morphic resonance is compatible with the idea of holographic reality as well. But Sheldrake's hypothesis does not require a holographic theory of brain function — since he does not think memory is confined to the brain itself.

Thus, Sheldrake's hypothesis in the scientific world creates a new context about brain functioning and consciousness. The M-fields, for example, presumably "bring order to randomness of synaptics, firings in the central nervous systems". The hypothesis of formative causation is exemplified in the following areas.

BEHAVIOUR

M-fields influence such behaviours like feeding, avoidance and mating. They pattern propagation of nerve impulses in a way that is partially ordered, partially indeterminate. The fields seem to structure behaviour in much the same way that they structure form, i.e. just as the field has the potential to restore wholeness in a damaged organism by regenerating cells of an injured part, it also regenerates behaviour, as a dog with an injured leg learns to walk differently. All such animal behaviour and even of insects who promptly learn from experience to adapt to new situations is an indication of striving to move towards wholeness, i.e. striving to complete a customary pattern. This kind of morphogenetic regulation and regeneration to reach behavioural goals does not raise any new fundamental principle even if it is unusual, since flexibility may be seen as an extension of the possibility inherent in M-fields by their very nature.

INSTINCT AND LEARNING

There is only a difference in degree between instincts and habits since both depend on morphic resonance, the former from countless previous individuals of the same species, and the latter mainly as past states of the same individual. Sheldrake goes on to suggest that memory is not localized necessarily at particular sites within the brain, and that learning may not be in the brain at all but "given directly from its past states by morphic resonance". Thus learning by an animal or a person comes from other members of its species who have already learned and were facilitated by morphic resonance with the emergence of the appropriate M-field from previous similar animals or persons. Or, a new field may come into being for the first time in the history of an individual or the first time ever. Psychologically there are several instances of this nature and Sheldrake reframes these long-standing problems in the light of morphic resonance, as follows:

(a) The idea of a cumulative experience or the collective unconscious of humankind such as those which include the archetypes of Carl Jung and others is also an indication of the pool of total memories stored beyond the storage capacity in the physical brain that receives signals from the total morphic resonance that is available. From the mechanistic viewpoint these speculations would appear to be nonsense although the mechanistic viewpoint on which most of the sciences are based is itself no more than speculative. Sheldrake's and the other scientists' hypothesis along with the use of proper imaginative kind of delving into ideas is in the direction of what Thomas Kuhn (1970) has termed "a paradigm shift" which means putting aside our assumptions on how the world works. This is in the beginning always difficult and uncomfortable today since the modern mechanistic science supposes that it has identified all of the major forces and fields at work in the world. If something is unexplained these theories suggest that with a little more information, research and knowledge the answers will naturally be produced in due course in the future. This is neither testible nor do we know if it has been possible.

(b) The hypothesis also allows for the explanation of paranormal events that seem to occur in various dimension of life and are unexplainable in terms of any non-physical principles. Psi as is commonly known may thus be inexplicably tied in part to the explanation by morphic resonance. At this level one may begin to enquire about the relationship between physics and consciousness, the mechanism of psychic healing, the phenomenon of dowsing, the remote viewing and other such areas which are being explored in great detail both in the West and in the USSR and eastern Europe. For example, psi or psychic phenomenon seems to occur when two states may at a time be little stressed, at the moment which is called the dynamic interval of being tuned into the same space. Such experiments have been carried out with rats quite often, as well as with insects whose behaviour is synchronized by creating a group bio-field within a unique electroencephalography (EEG) spectrum. The idea or concept of "ethnic brain" and "supra-ethnic brain" has been brought into existence through these studies suggesting that an individual field represents a "neuron" that belongs to the general ethnic field. These people are able to forecast and predict accurately about events that occur sometimes in the future. This is a case, that has also been noted in what has been called the Australian "dream time". In this case, whenever an expedition wants to go across Australia through some unknown territory any object such as a piece of cloth or other remnant of a previous expedition, when this is brought in close proximity to the aborigine he seems to get into a consciousness by this stimulus or code which brings him in touch with the entire route of the previous expedition. Thus he is able to take this new expedition into a journey of the unknown without his having been there, or a reference to a map or other such devices. Such influence and knowledge about the many tribal groups all over the world is well known and yet unexplained.

There is the interesting case of a tribe in West Africa, the Dogon tribe, whose traditional ritual and worship include the mythology of people coming from a distant star today called Sirius. It is only in this century that scientists discovered that it was a binary system, i.e. it had another companion star that is not visible to the naked eye. It is inexplicable that this primitive tribe has knowledge about an invisible star, that its mythology of long-standing tells about people coming from the same star to give this information, and that despite the bare technology with which they survive in West Africa. Whether the *śāman*, or its equivalent, caught this knowledge through a potential state of consciousness (very likely a way of travel), or whether some people actually "came through" whatever modes of transport, is difficult to say. But obviously one has to evolve fundamentally different perspectives to be able to account for the phenomenon, since the currently available hypothesis is totally inadequate. Even a plant which is chemically injured, or given a toxic agent in water, reacts to such a state and communicate, not only to other parts of it but to other plants about its very reaction to danger.

The case of dowsing, to detect hidden materials such as water with a divining rod, is an ancient practice in all traditional societies.

There is a correlation between this state of mind, or what is called a correlation in the neuro-physiological low frequency states, and successful dowsers. There are, thus, various wavelengths that seem to correlate with such a phenomenon, or even thought forms and structures created by the imagination that gives insights to other persons in tune with these fields. Then there is the contact of human mental systems to inanimate systems — and even laser beams — as are affected by psychic activity; these are under experiment vis-à-vis the psycho-energetic effects that may be trained unconsciously (Mishra 1985).

All these explanations and origins of new forms, and behaviours in subjective experiences are in some way compatible with certain of the world views available in different religions and philosophies such as the following (Sheldrake 1983).

MODIFIED MATERIALISM

Just as material particles are reconsidered as forms of energy, so could this concept be extended to include M-fields. Consciousness could then be defined in terms of the effects of M-fields rather than stored in the brain. But this concept implies no purpose beyond the satisfaction of biological and social needs.

THE CONSCIOUS SELF

Here, consciousness is an additional causative principle that enters into the activities of M-fields and yet stays aloof so that it may choose between alternative possibilities in terms of its chosen ability. Memory would thus be explained as having direct access of the conscious self — to its past states — rather than to the brain or M-fields. And both these and the first concept of novelty and creativity in plant, mineral and human life may remain accounted for due purely to chance or to a transcendent creative agency.

THE CREATIVE UNIVERSE

This theory supposes the presence of a creative immanence at least in life forms through hierarchic creative states or levels. It explains evolutionary creativity but no creation of the universe itself which would be evolving continuously without any purpose and direction, more like the other two hypotheses.

TRANSCENDENT REALITY

This supposes a conscious agent that transcends what it creates; and, cause and purpose would then be explainable not in terms of a specific goal but it would be its own goal since by itself it would be complete. There would be a more or less limited wholeness or organism at all levels whose unit of which it depended and from which they were ultimately derived. The physical body may thus be seen in this context of consciousness also (holistic awareness), so that there is an inherent wisdom of the body which is therefore in tune with, or vibrating to the natural frequency and the wavelength of consciousness that is immanent in all of the elemental forms. This is what allows for a total or completely healthy body and brain system, at one with the flow of life and with the consciousness which is both transcendent and immanent, one and at the same time.

Unfortunately, current cultural attitudes and limited hypotheses in all our developmental programmes have ignored these ancient insights of much meaning. Take the notion of a subtle and causal body, or the idea of *saṁskāra*; the latter is a thought that has been repeated for long and which results in actions that are further repeated for a thousand years. In this context, personality is an aggregate of *saṁskāra*, and without such an awareness to have little choice. But in this ever-changing process, it is attention, awareness or consciousness — that allows for flexibility in thought and action. This is where the opportunity for choice becomes available, to undo or dismantle through repeated thought, that is consciously, i.e. earlier *saṁskāra*. This is to reverse the process instead of thinking one's self as always the same in some imaginary or conceptual way. This is how, unconsciously, we become what we think, and thereby effect every tissue in a body which is in a constant state of change and repair. To get into another dimension of choice and control — by choiceless awareness — one needs for one thing, to unlearn, the concept of linear time.

4

A Study of the Past and the Concept of Time

A STUDY of the past is an attempt to trace human development by recording and interpreting events of human experience in an evolutionary–chronological sequence. But these interpretations of human activity somehow become convincingly real. It is often forgotten that these are only conceptual interpretations of events, known rather fragmentarily or partially; and this, too, limited by specific viewpoints. In being unconscious of such limitations, the outpourings of these studies into the overall educational system continue to reinforce a fragmentary view of human experience. The given area is linked to a deeper examination of the way we know, acquire and interpret knowledge in general. This means, as is well known by philosophers, to look deeply into that epistemology of the knowledge of the past which is governed by one's perceptual, conceptual and metaphysical notions (Malik 1968). History, for example, is commonly believed to be a set of facts which one simply puts in order, by some accepted canons of knowledge, as if it were an "objective" viewpoint. But is this really so? All perceptions of past events are from the point of view of the existential present. The viewer and what is viewed are inextricably bound to each other. The notion of "objective" or detached history, in fact of any knowledge, especially in the historical and social sciences, is a misleading notion. All ideas are continuously changing in terms of the overall growth of knowledge in general (Postle 1976).

Thus, historical knowledge is continuously being rewritten in terms of our present perceptions, of how we want to mould the contemporary society. In fact this is how a study of the past is frequently used to justify each social group's, or nation's, political and economic demands. A study of the past plays a very crucial role in contemporary society since all ideological–political movements, whether conservative or liberal, use — and more often distort — historical evidence. History thus becomes a kind of contemporary mythology. To give a very simple example, the 1857 event has been variously called; an army "mutiny" if one happens to be British. We leave aside the fact of what actually may have happened since the event itself has many testimonies and evidences which are incorporated variously by histories themselves.

Again, a general notion is that a group of people, whether a small or a large entity as a nation — which itself is a concept — has a single history. But it is obvious that there is no single history since each group tends to view a particular event from its own viewpoint. In fact, even within a single more or less homogeneous group, whether this is a linguistic or social group, the same event is incorporated and interpreted in different ways. The historian may claim that it takes all this into account to produce a compo- site and objective description. But this arises again from an idea of current state of perceptions of reality in general and historical research methodology which may change at any time — however sound these may appear for the moment. Moreover, these methods are inseparable from a comprehension and interpretation of the past event itself, that is, the past events create the present notions as well. Human perception and human action within the framework of consciousness are inseparable.

Field workers in anthropology and sociology who have studied various societies can easily testify that divergent histories are maintained by different subgroups even at the village level either as remembrances or even as living experiences. Clearly it is our consciousness and action which keep producing various images. These keep changing or perpetually sifting and shifting the norms and values whereby the present and the past are totally intertwined. There is no discreet separation of the past from the present, for a unified sense of knowledge of the past has a beginning and existence in the present, moment to moment. This viewpoint has been presented often enough not only by philosophers but by philosophers of history as well. Obviously, it has had little effect in the accounts of historical writing that are presented to the lay public or even in the academic discipline both at the school and university educational systems.

The aim of research into human history is with an intention to broaden human experience, of which recorded history is a very minute fragment that is known to us. Even unrecorded events as revealed by archaeological and other means, the knowledge we gain about man is meagre. The knowledge we have is in bits and pieces. If it continues to grow and enlarge, it is because of the widening of our perceptions due to scientific developments in other disciplines. Moreover, it has also enlarged because of changing conceptual models that govern what we know, since the way we know sets the limits of our perceptions. To illustrate, it is taken for granted that the cultural evolutionary model placed within detailed linear sequences of developmental studies is a close approximation of reality. This view is interrelated closely to the notion of development and progress; ideas which arose from early colonial viewpoints. These considered various non-European societies at different primitive levels of existence on technological and economic grounds and therefore also at sociocultural and metaphysical levels. The division of human history into history and prehistory (defined by the dividing line of writing) itself is a clear evidence of the intellectual illusion of the past such as the secondary place given to oral tradition which, for example, is of such importance in the maintenance of India's cultural tradition. But by ignoring it arises the notion of India's not having an idea of historicity, or being ahistorical in nature.

The notion of an unbroken linear sequences is very often used for both our individual and social existences. The basic idea behind this is the notion of time which appears to follow one narrow path, based only on fixed points that are interconnected in terms of cause and effect. This fundamental notion of unbroken causation, that certain events exist because of certain previous events, is another total misconception of not only understanding various cultures but the construction of reality in general. This kind of simplification is a very common feature for the understanding of human history and in fact the outer universe on which we impose our notions, of such rather limited patterns. A clear definition needs to be kept in mind, between say the landscape and the lines that we draw on our map. It is well to remember that the map and the lines are superimpositions or a systematic organization of the vast complexity called reality.

Cyclical time is composed of rhythmic patterns like the seasons, the phases of the moon, the tides, day and night. Time and history are inclusive in this cyclic notion for the idea of simultaneity forms the background of this world view. It accepts the conventions of historic time within this rotating wheel in which the past, present and future are concurring. It is only the continuous present of the "now". In this "time" there are many dimensions but these are simultaneous, not sequential. The notion of a linear view of time has become so ingrained in modern man, that at first it seems almost impossible to grasp any notion of cyclic time, or a view of morality which is not based on cause and effect. This idea of linear time subscribes to the notion of continuous change, and in which the major concern is always with the past and with the future; so that, the least substantial part is the present which not only becomes impossible to perceive but also to grasp. Therefore, any understanding of the present which requires multidimensional interrelatedness, of the mutual influence of simultaneous events on a particular or specific process or patterns is difficult to comprehend, if it is to be based on a linear explanation of cause and effect.

However, to the particle physicist it is fairly evident, from the work done in quantum theory that sequential causation is an insufficient theory to explain the behaviour of subatomic matter (Capra 1980). At this level, certainly, events separated in space and time, without any possibility of a connection, interact and are correlated in a manner that any detailed causal explanation is inadequate. Quantum theory has therefore far-reaching implications, in terms of understanding the fundamental universal laws which relate to matter and its movements. This is related to any development of an overall world view within which there is a need to accommodate historical thinking, and from similar other systems of related disciplines. For instance, many events are explained away merely in terms of "coincidences" — or that these occur by mere "chance". The statement ignores the extraordinary conjunction of events which frequently occur, but are merely explained away by the word "coincidence" since it does not fit into our current linear notions of cause and effect. Certain non-European cultures that have different world views understand better the occurrences of such events within the framework of cyclical world views, without labelling these as mere "chance", or taking them as some superstitious stuff. One other reason for not taking such random events seriously is that even in the so-called exact sciences verification without quantification is exceedingly unlikely to be taken into account. Given that explanations are often at a superficial level, the deep structures of our perceptions of reality are not taken into account. These latter insights are of such fundamental nature that they lie below superficial conscious- ness. It is like taking the ground we walk on, or the gravity which governs our every action for granted, and still not taking it into account as it concerns one's behaviour. In other words, our outdated hidden belief systems and which we are so familiar with, unconsciously control our view of reality and the method of investigation. In short, what we attempt to view, or perceive, historically is governed by motivations which are culturally conditioned.

Thus, whenever we attempt to grasp reality without a deeper reflection it only reveals itself in our interpretations in terms of what we already know. This reflects on not only the inability, but limitations of knowledge. It does not allow us to explain events, leave aside being able to take into account a description of reality as perceived by other cultures and civilizations than our own.

This is why in this limited, Western-oriented understanding of human history we often view other cultures and civilizations, both contemporary and of the past, as if "those" were different from us — we who have a rational, scientific understanding in terms of this notion of sequential cause–effect phenomenal explanations. At any rate, this is but one viewpoint — in other words the knowledge of history is no more than a contemporary, a limited angle of vision both in its individual or its social dimensions. A great many cultures have a viewpoint of reality which is "non-historical" in the sense of our definition of history in a way. In many cultures this enterprise of history is encompassed within the scale of cosmic time wherein a human lifetime is insignificant. Consequently, the recording of words and action in this context of modern historical consciousness seems a self-defeating enterprise (Malik 1975).

According even to the current Big Bang theory, the universe was created at least 13 billion years ago, and now contains billions of galaxies, each of which contains billions of solar systems like ours; the thought should make contemporary man, even for a moment, contemplate the vastness of these temporal dimensions. But then contemporary history is closely bound to the notion of progress and the technological advances. These have however arisen from this notion of separation, such as the domination of man over nature. It is as if the historian stands aside without any participation in order to record human events. As said earlier, such recording and writing of history, so also in other areas of human endeavour, involves a participation of the scholar that brings about a change in other parts of human reality. It is very clear that the very act of participation itself changes what is to be perceived; even the words we use are powerful agents in bringing about changes. The universe is a participatory universe, that is very clear to many scientists who deal with life at this metaphysical level. So the notion of a detached and objective observer is, in a way, shirking from a responsibility (and therefore contributes also) of the power to change and create the present state of our civilization. The present hypothetical proposition whereby experience is interpreted within a confrontation duality — of the self and others — is a major cause of the crisis of civilization.

Thus, any revolutionary change that everybody intends to bring about has only to come through well-intentioned efforts by changing or transforming the world view at the core of the self; and, thereby, that which has governed contemporary society and its ways of systematizing the past and present. This is not to suggest that the discipline of history is not scientific, rather that one go beyond superficiality; that there should be more rigour and precision in ways of knowing and verifying knowledge in the sense of examining its deep philosophical foundations. It is to make the discipline concrete (most people believe, that to turn philosophical is to be vague or abstract) rather than to let it remain a partial and distorted projection of human experience from only one viewpoint — it becoming the fountainhead of a great deal of destruction. Accepting subjectivity is to accept the responsibility for what one does to self, as to others. This spells both rigour and imagination, as also bestows the sense of responsibility towards the present politico-economic events. History will always, as even in the case of knowing the continuous present, remain partial; distorted projections of our state of mind whereby we observe the universe, and have fleeting glimpses of fragments of reality. This is no cause of pessimism or despair but an indication of more responsibility in terms of what little we know. Accepting limitations is one of the first steps to go beyond limitations. It is to move towards explanations that arise from other dimensions within Consciousness.

As summary, then, in discussing the past we need not differentiate knowledge into history in the academic sense which includes the arbitrary divisions of archaeology and anthropology or other divisions. We may take knowledge of the past to be both in terms of general society in relationship to nature, mythologies and even where personal relationships are governed. The past of the person is no different from the past of wider historical knowledge since both are intertwined in the social and cultural systems. Again, it is widely held that there is objective history separate from a personal or subjective history either at the individual level or the viewpoint of the people themselves and their own historical developments. It is almost as if some kind of an objective history is possible as an outsider as opposed to the subjective ideas of the people or the individual himself. This certainly does not ensure that there is objectivity in one viewpoint and subjectivity in the other. In fact, any viewpoint is subjective in nature, and this is especially true more so where man is examining his own nature or the society around him. Of course, at least in physics if not in other sciences, it is getting clearer that there is no absolute objectivity bereft of any, if not conscious, then unconscious involvement of the observer with that which is being observed. In the dynamics of continuous change, within which principles of the universe and human societies exist, there is a continuous interaction of this kind. This is a fundamental aspect of the functioning of the universe, of a continuous movement, of creation and destruction in what to us often looks like disorder and chaos since we see it from a limited viewpoint.

Any knowledge of the past, even individual experiential knowledge is instantly converted into signs and symbols of various kinds in the form of thought so that it becomes a way to comprehend the external world. It is part of thought processes to take conceptualized knowledge of events and processes to be reality itself, rather than to remember that it is only a coded symbol of the actual. This kind of comprehension in compartmentalized or fragmented manner is the same when we view not only the past but the present and the future as well. The way of our knowledge is the same since it is an interaction in terms of categories based on our perceptual, conceptual and metaphysical notions of the universe. Perception by means of sense organs is in fact governed by conceptual notions which, in the mind, in turn are governed by deeper unconscious memories, and the received metaphysical ideas.

The notion of what we normally call "fact", and which appears to be self-existent, is only so because there is consensus on the issue. It is because of a common agreement that a "fact" is taken to be self-evident. In the European world, at one time, there was a general agreement that the earth was flat which at that point of time was taken to be an axiomatic truth (or that at one time it was the centre of the solar system). Yet even though there was consensus, these so-called facts were in time to be totally reversed. Once again, an intuitive insight — that of Einstein – transformed everything, almost totally, and the Newtonian universe was gone. Relativity has become an intrinsic part, today, of both specialized and general knowledge. Is it for this the universe has changed, or is it that transformations take place because the perspectives which have changed, almost as if overnight? Actual or factual situation of a certain event is itself the result of various ways of knowing and interpreting evidence, leave aside the labelling of it. The past is extremely difficult to restructure except in terms of probability statements from one viewpoint or other although sometimes it may even not have existed at all — which a later perspective may reveal to us. Even the individual's own personal history is a reconstruction of limited, yet sharp memories of certain events which he "believes" took place and therefore became cause or reason for his own life and autobiography.

Thus, knowledge of the past is governed by existing viewpoints, i.e. the contemporary viewpoints of the past. All history is contemporary history, and these are used as explanatory devices or justifications for the various objectives of present society. Both individual and society continuously use this historical knowledge or memories in symbolized form for justification of actions in the present. In fact, the same historical knowledge is used for projections, for various plans and notions about the future itself. All future projections arise from these kinds of explanations, or even notions of what ought to be and should be for the benefit of individual, society or nation. Notions of the past are projected into the future out of fear and anxiety in order not to repeat painful or other events. Thought continuously moves between these two dimensions, the past and the future, both in fact being the same. Since from the viewpoint of the present these are only concepts about the past which cannot directly be known and the future, which once again becomes a projection of the past itself. The present is therefore only a modification of the structural notions about the past. There is no actual future or the past which we often seem to project and imagine but tend to take abstraction to be real (*fig.* 4.1).

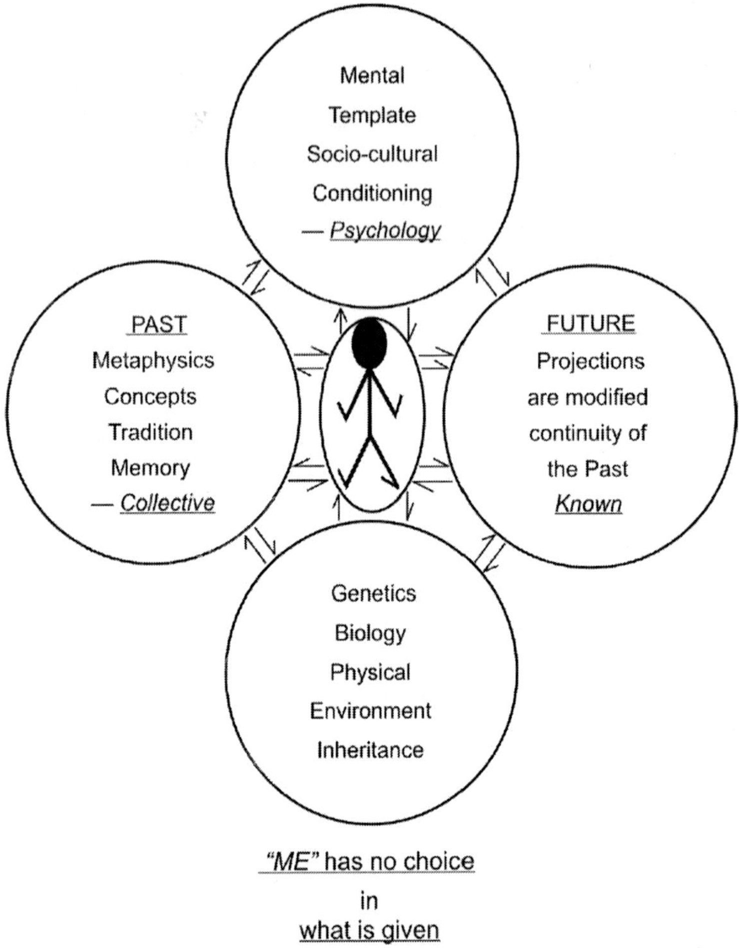

fig.4.1: Future and past tend to take abstraction as real

Explanation to *fig.* 4.1

The individual "me" or "I" is made of many variables and functions relationally and is interrelated and interdependent. There is no independent autonomous self which is a fallacy, since the notion of the self has arisen from conditioning in the given socio-cultural set up in which this physical somatic "self" is born. But the brain washing is so strong that the non-independent notion of the "me" at first seems absurd. The uniqueness that is there, is within a certain given psychosomatic set up or within a relatively already given situation within which one is born in. Even physically one is governed by factors of (i) environment, (ii) Biology, (iii) genetic inheritance of DNA and RNA, (iv) socio-cultural inheritance and (iv) All the elements which are already given.

Given the above statement stated simply, this somatic structure is functioning on its own, from the time the ovum is fertilized, without the knowledge of "me" which gets created in the given socio-cultural set up. He/she doesn't even know or is aware of how this is happening, say functioning of the heart, liver, kidney, etc. that is, this bundle of trillions of cells with all the glands, hormones, ductless glands, etc. One does not know as to how these are coordinated, breathing, digestion and so on. One is only aware of those organs when there is discomfort and pain. All of this is programmed physically and mentally. If one gives attention to all this, one will see that everything is happening on its own, it is all a happening! The "me" is only an image given by society, expressed in the language one is brought up in, yet that "me as thought, as "me", as language functions very strongly mentally that is run, by it, which Gurdieff calls the "little professor" sitting in head, from age of 7, it passes judgements, evaluations and so on which form the "ego" or "me" and one is subservient to that voice, thought following the Cartesian dictum of "I think therefore I am" little realizing that "thought" is "me", there is no separate "me"! So you and I arise out of a collective system that conditions one, giving a false image of a "me". But this "me" has no choice, one is an unconscious robot, an automaton.

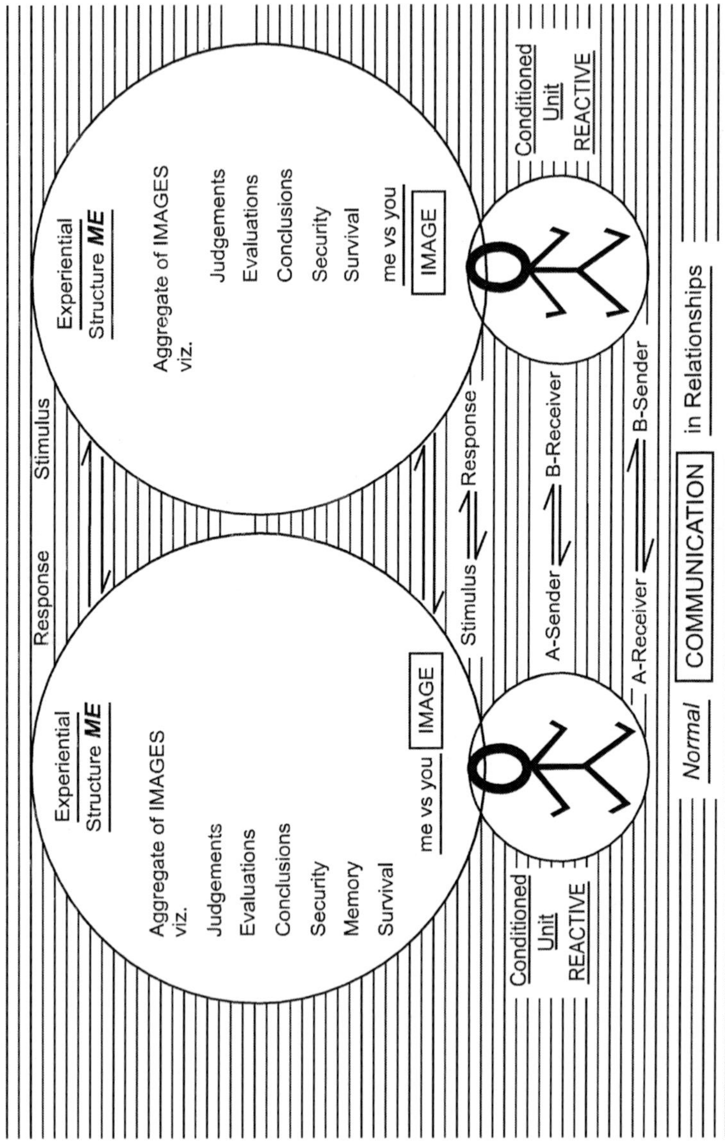

fig. 4.2: Anatomy of communication

Explanation to *fig.* 4.2

How does one know what one knows? How does one think, and what to think? So, what is knowing?

In interpersonal communication, or even at public levels receiver and sender are already programmed, and are already conditioned. At both the individual and public level, all communication arises from pre-conceived conceptual interpretations, i.e. arise from the socio-cultural images set into the system from the earliest upbringing, and from before as *sanskars*. The image or role models arise at the socializing processes within the larger cultural context which is further based on the world views. The images, say, of oneself as parent, child, uncle, husband–wife, teacher, director, etc. are social roles which one identifies with, as one's identity because the role or act one is putting one is programmed. There is no choice here even if one defies it, this imposition. Communication in everyday "normal" living, especially in relationships, takes place according to the structure of the "me" consisting of several images. These then consist of surface and deep memories that are stored interpretations of experiences. All experiences are interpretations that hide the experience because the labelling of these is in terms of known data. One has been brought up to label and name experiences linguistically. That is why no two people agree on an event or experience as it is governed by the conceptual framework within which one functions. That is why there are different interpretations and debates about "what is". Each individual and this larger socio-cultural system comprise of mental concepts. Therefore the world is a projection of mental states, there are statements of the world as concepts, and not "actual" or real as primary experiences not diluted by interpretations. Thus even physical experiences of the senses, the phenomenal world, are manifested by the conditions often in linguistic or languaging, of utterances.

Hence there are is one's head a widespread levels of judgements, evaluation, conclusions, hopes, wishes, resentments, regrets, etc. often in order to maintain one's identity which one thinks one is, especially for its survival and to seek psychological security even if garbed variously in term of material well-being. There are mental agitations that appear as defensive/offensive behavioural patterns, including feeling of guilt, self-pity, lack of self-worth, seeking approval-attention. In short, this "person" or group who basically is insecure psychically tries to from this state of insecurity, wants security. There are attempts to "become" or reach a certain imagined state where one finally feels contented and settled – usually approved and accepted by the imagined society he/she imagines, or images. In an insecure world, ephemeral physical world, with social images that are changing constantly, how can this false conceptual me, become psychologically secure? The very fact of in insecure me and the changing universe, seeking security and permanency is the cause of insecurity. It is the cause of alienation, suffering and the present crisis of he individual and human civilization.

Again, even the present knowledge of any event includes the same processes as enumerated above, that is perception of the external world — once again — a conceptualization rather than "fact". The present in fact becomes equally elusive in this dual movement of the mind from the "past" into the "future" and on its way viewing what it calls the category of the "present". It is thus a totally false position to claim, any real actual knowing of the past, or the present, or the future, except in symbolic expressions of "what is". These three dimensions are nothing but abstract notions of what we presume to be seeing, listening or receiving within this bodily instrument, including the computerized brain system. This kind of knowledge of "reality", seen from this point of view, is to that extent "unreal" and "illusory". A concept of an experience cannot be mistaken for the experience itself, nor will it ever produce that experience. As is often said, the menu is not food itself. The way the world is today, it is as if human beings have lost this innate capacity to be even aware that the essence of experience is missing; that we are chewing concepts rather than experiencing the eating of food. Beyond metaphors this is actually the case even in daily life, when food is eaten as memory, as impressions, it is not a fresh experience; it is as if one is chewing the cud most of the time. To move out of these deep grooves of thought would seem to require a great deal of unlearning (*fig.* 4.2).

5

Learning and Communication

Learning Is Unlearning

THE manner in which learning is being considered here is substantively other than some commonly held notions. Briefly, learning as seen in education systems and society in general is basically a process of the accumulation of information. There is an ever increasing specialization of diversified information, and it is easily accessible because of sophisticated technology. But such is its pace that even a specialized worker cannot keep up with his own field. As a consequence, he sometimes begins to concentrate on even narrower areas of research. The same is true for all walks of life, such as administrative departments that are organized under various specialized sections, or as in large-scale industrial units. And this rather mechanical manner is like the running of an army organization where different units perform their duty as commanded, with little knowledge of the overall picture —perhaps justifiable in the contest of a battle strategy. But all such approaches are inappropriate in terms of human psychology and a healthy society, the human being depersonalized and alienated from his work and relationship leave aside any comprehension of a total perception of life.

This kind of fragmentation in the educational system is equally obvious if one even for a moment stands aside to look, as it were as an outsider, in all of the systems. Sociocultural learning is conditioned or what we call learning, is, too often, a mere mechanical form of ritualistic repetition. This is a drilling of information into the fresh minds of the young, whether it is a parrot-like repetition or some other form of sophisticated knowledge of science in a specialized way. It has little to do even with its proclaimed aims of education, far from bringing in the quality of life which allows for the capacity of an individual to think for himself. Thus learning, as at present, is not a genuine education, and even in functional societal day-to-day living, thought itself is the extension of a technological dimension with a paradigm that supports the notion of this survival of social existence. The "survival" philosophy is a carry over from prehistoric times. It amounts to dragging useless genetic traits of biological evolution. Clearly this misdirected overspecialization has become very destructive. The more this lopsided growth, the more there the raising of slogans "of tremendous progress", one which is a defensive cover for the fact of human kind going downhill. The error needs to be corrected now, if it is perhaps not already too late.

On the other hand, and that even biologically speaking, the process of true learning is an essential ingredient of healthy, holistic evolutionary growth. It is part of the ongoing life process. The biological foundation of learning seems to have been forgotten in an overconcern with the mere mechanical or repetitive way of life that has overtaken the existence of the human species. Biological survival has become an abstraction unrelated to life. Learning requires the giving up of outdated ideas. What is normally called "learning", even in every day life, is the name for those unconscious habits whereby each individual or group lives his life of physio-social survival. But this is not a truly human view of learning, such "survival" — being at the cost of others. It is no learning — in the holistic sense — when given that there are certain painful experiences and fearing that the old ways will disappear, one adapts to new situations simply in order to continue the same in another garb. Also, what one today calls educational learning is often the mere accumulation of information about events. Such is being used as a lever for power, for dominance. Moreover, we imagine, if we put all of this expanding knowledge together it will automatically reveal a picture or solve certain problems. Actually, such informational growth is within the old paradigms. What we are doing is to mechanically perpetuate many old ideas — what is already known — either in a simple or sophisticated form. All this present learning is part of "survival"– mechanical paradigm, not creative learning.

So, our lives are governed by ideas which are complete abstractions, namely, the label or name given to the individual, family, a larger aggregate or social group called nation, or even a group of nations. All these are conceptual formulations that have become crucial as images. Their survival — of label, sign, symbol, name, etc. — has become a must, at any expense. This is why we observe that human life has come to be deemed the least important, not to speak of animal and plant life. It is much too evident that in this century hundreds of millions of people have been killed systematically and human kind is preparing to kill itself a fifty times over! It sounds a bit strange, this quantification, though it puts forth clearly the mechanical way of thinking and being. In short, it is the perpetuation of ideas of quantity which dominates our philosophy of life — an unconscious one. In other words, we kill for the sake of an idea or a symbol, whether it be a flag or a name or some other form of outward appearance, say clothes; and all of which are cultural or social symbols. For this, man is ready to kill his own near and dear ones; human beings who claim to love their children train them to kill themselves and other human beings. Though these endeavours seem so apparently horrendous, yet we continue the game, especially so the leaders of power groups who egg and incite others to join a suicidal game. Almost all of human kind appears caught in this perversity today, albeit with a pretense of survival or the illusion of swimming towards a brighter future! The chasing of this continuously receding mirage is a utopia that is beyond one's grasp. We are not only putting the carrot before the donkey but also beating it in the behind! Mankind is doing this to itself almost non-stop, not realizing the deadly consequences of chasing the illusion of an old, outmoded paradigm whose time and utility are long since past.

The consequences, because of this specialization, are that a fraction of the brain area today is functionally tyrannizing our existence. It leaves three-fourths of the brain to deteriorate, which may be rejuvenated, were the lopsided growth to be corrected. This in turn requires an awareness of the said misguided conditioning, which by itself is the first step which will rejuvenate the dormant brain, so essential for holistic functioning. The total brain has been in existence for the entire evolutionary growth of man and yet has been ignored for thousands of years. The first step, therefore, towards learning is to be aware of what learning is not all about. It is with this awareness, through one's own efforts, that one may begin to unlearn all those habits and patterns which have been governing our life. It is only when one learns to acknowledge how much one does not know, to say, "I do not know", instead of seeking an identity or taking a position of "I know", that the process of learning begins. As children, we are all eager to see and learn since the world appears as a wonderful open book, full of new activity. But conditioned beings lose that ability of learning and liveliness, as we cling to memories, the known.

In other words, the learning process requires the discarding of a great deal of what one may call "grime" that continues to accumulate on the mirror of the mind. In this "polishing" of the mirror, will emerge perhaps a truer reflection once the cleaning process begins. The human brain, and this is not referring to an individual brain, in general through generations of racial, biological and cultural inheritance has become cluttered with so much of irrelevant facts and useless knowledge — for a limited purpose — that entropy or self-destruction has happened. The learning processes can only begin to take place with a drastic clearing up. It is like a closed room in which things are continuously being accumulated and dust is gathering on windows and doors, which do not allow for any light to enter. It is in this darkness of a prison of one's own creation that mankind seeks freedom, or begins to build dreams — out of neuroses — of a beautiful future. In this attempt man seems to think that the dreams are in fact Reality. He makes them, with this ever-increasing movement of anxiety, into a nightmare. It increases his perplexity with every attempt to clear up, believing that he seems to be enjoying the coming of a bright future. For example, he continues to live in that blackhole of a prison, with artificial light, to keep cleaning the dust from one object and transferring it to another. Or he replaces one object by another, and pretends to cover one object from the underlying dirt, by beautifully dressing it.

Thus, he goes on to self indulge, even while his deepest unconscious knows that there is no real freedom in all these attempts; that these are only varied and different motions within his — the room as a prison — dreams or nightmares. He makes himself believe that change or "progress" is taking place; and, that "one day" that ungraspable "one day" will finally emerge when there will be light in the room. A sad, false, pitiable condition. This too in self-wrought knots. Man gets caught in these knots more and more while pretending to free himself; imagining that with every attempt he will finally be free "one day". But that "one day" has stretched to 5,000 years of civilization. In our own lives these imaginary adventures seem to be still continuing.

The myth is of reaching the goal by the next elusive generation which will have gained that utopia, knowing fully well that utopias are never gained; that it is only one utopia which replaces another, like a continuously receding mirage. To take an example, the First World War (and it has a strange paradox of a slogan and which has continued to prevail even till today) that it was a "war to end all wars", and "one day" like the Second World War was to be the same. And, of course, all the other wars after that when more weapons were used and, more people killed than the earlier wars in which European or Western powers were involved. Living in these abstractions is so totally tragic, because it is the situation of being oblivious of a fact which makes for the present way of life, of a world order. One cannot fight in order to bring peace and harmony. Since fear, anger, hatred and greed mainly form the basis of such endeavours, these shake the very foundations of civilization. As long as they are left unattended to, there simply cannot be any positive progress or the beginnings of the truer learning.

The statements above indicate of how much unlearning, or

how much awakening from long slumber, is required by us. A start has to be made by a few or even by one individual human being. The learning process is the discarding process in everyday life. We all know how, to the accumulated waste and dust of centuries of memories and ideas, each man clings, in some strange kind of a desperation. Shall we say, perhaps, in a more accurate way, that it is a partial memory, of the total memory pool that is trying to maintain itself in some very devious way through man for its own survival, rather than of living a full life, in totality of what may be called experiential moments of Here and Now, though using knowledge or memories as and when required. But this is not the case at all. The futility of this normal kind of endeavour becomes apparent in such rare moments of each individual's life when by chance a ray of light enters into this darkness and gives an insight into the essential Being or Beingness of life, which is within us and very closeby. However, these rare moments even though these are real in the experience of each individual, are taken to be unreal, or hallucinations, or something extremely difficult to grasp since the old habit of being in darkness is what one has become so used to, it is taken to be real. This is what causes sheer lethargy that preventing one from clearing up all of the grime accumulated on the mind's mirror.

The first impact, when a man comes out of darkness or even as he receives a ray of light, is certainly either startling or it blinds one. It is even more difficult to discard the dream or nightmare which one had taken to be reality. This amounts to the dropping of old habits or that which is already known. This unlearning process is necessary to relearn from life, as a process of daily life. This is a biological characteristic and necessity. It has no goals or ends by itself. The learning process itself is the essence of life, a life of freedom from the past, or the known, in all its dimensions that ancient philosophies and their modern interpreters are never tired of telling mankind. Closely linked with this learning process, or the ending of time in terms of presentation of analysis, is the essence of communication (Krishnamurti and Bohm 1985).

What Is True Communication?

True communication is not merely a verbal exchange. It is a total exchange-experience of all of the sensory perceptions. For example, when there is an exchange of words between two people it is not only the tone and intonation that count but also the whole structure of the other gestures of the body and the various facial expressions and so on that get communicated. Even in the case of the written word each one of us has an intuitive grasp of the hidden meaning that is being conveyed. Often, it is possible to state whether there is sincerity in the written word or mere superficial play of words by the author. Apparently, there are other means and dimensions, or there is an intangible media, which allows us to grasp the essence of what is being stated. In the case of one's own self these dimensions become known to us if we stop; to be aware of this process of communication. Ordinarily, communication takes place at two levels: one, the verbal superficial exchange of words, and the other is the hidden meaning which we are consciously or unconsciously expressing. Most communication is governed by the accepted norms of economic, social and cultural patterns. The superficial structure or rituals and expressions of external behaviour seem to dominate most of one's life. This is in contradiction to the great deal of inner urges and feelings and emotions which for some reason or the other are not expressed even partially because of sometimes real and most often imaginary fears of social pressures or lack of receiving approval. We hold back or restrain an authentic or sincere expression of ourselves. Thus, in this way, true relationship and communication is kept in abeyance.

Normal communication takes place in a conditioned form of knowledge, in which one is brought up. It is thus that various forms of "social understanding" tends to be perpetuated in what one calls tradition, that is "the way it is" in a society. In other words the consensus interpretation of what life is actually about, not what we experience directly and intuitively. This kind of understanding from which communication arises is based on a deep conditioning which has prevailed for several millennia. It is of a conceptual nature and not even concepts that each individual

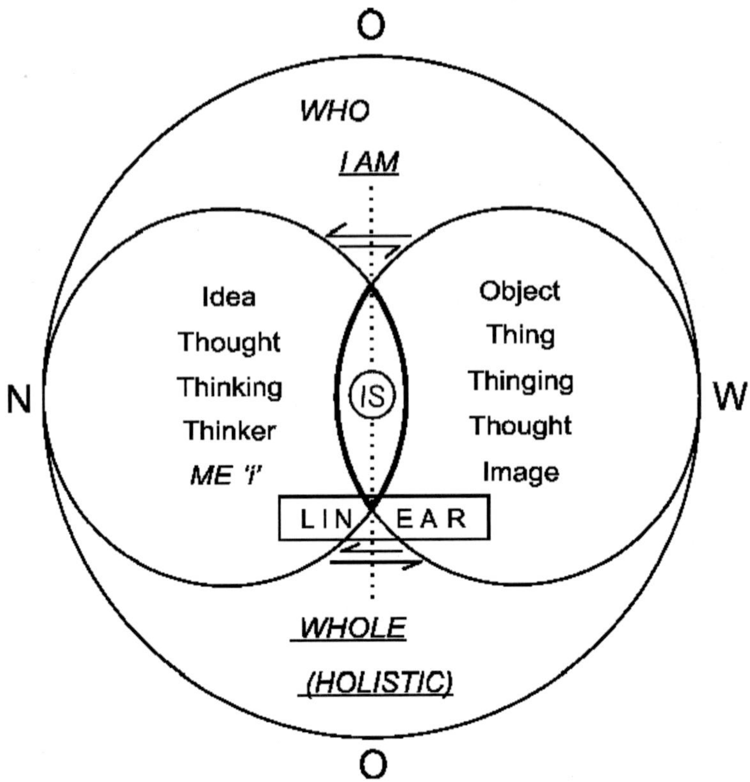

fig. 5.1: Holistic now

Explanation to *fig*. 5.1

Given the above simply and briefly stated premise, in this manner, the figure illustrates that both sender and receiver are functioning within the same imaginary context. How can then actual communication take place within this reactive stimulus- response, conditioned state? This is living in an unconscious state presuming that this is actual/real. In this context even the senses of taste, smell, hearing, seeing are functioning within interpretative thinking. The hearing, for instance, is not the same as listening, seeing in mere looking and not seeing as an insight. Similarly one is seeing, hearing, tasting, smelling, feeling, coming from previous interpretations of the known memories or database. It is a movement of thoughts memories from known to the known or from the familiar to the familiar as recorded in the memories or database. In this manner of "living" is actually so-called living of memories. Even these are misinterpretations in different language garbs governed by psychological notions of attention and approval which the situations require. This is why the person (latin *personae*) is a mask, that is one is playing many roles which one often assumes to be a real identity. It becomes so real and serious that one is ready to die for it!

In short, at all levels there is a false sense of communication, more meetings and discussions with the hope of a solution or resolution. This is like a dog chasing its own tail. There are no fresh experience moment to moment as perhaps as children (child-like) one knew. We are so used to chewing the cud, that is experiences are all the time interpreted. that no first hand fresh experience, even in taste, smell recedes into the background. To move out of these grooves, one has first to be aware of these false assumptions and be ready to drop these old ways or be ready to let go or unlearn in order to be alive and feel fresh once more. It is to unbecome, to delete he garbage, the baggage of reduntant words, thoughts and emotions. It's a movement from the head to the heart, or to integrate or balance the two and become one whole (holistic) once again. This is to move beyond fragmentation, that is all-pervasive in the world today. To be whole means to be Holy once again.

True communication is not merely a verbal exchange. It is a total exchange experientially with all sensory perceptions, beyond the conditioned self, a non-verbal state. This requires for the person to go within, to face him/herself, to face the question of "who am I?" This requires deeper knowing the structure of the "me", of thoughts, of notion of becoming and of being.

thinks for himself. Therefore, whatever is communicated is once again a social symbolic interpretation both by the sender of the signal and the receiver, both at the verbal and non-verbal levels. For example, if in a group of people, if one asks each one to answer at that very instant a reaction to one word, say what "money" means to them, each one at the first instance, without trying to give the meaning, will come up with his or her own first associations, or images in the context of his or her individual wants and wishes.

Thus, to one person what will come to mind (with the association of money) may be a desire to buy a car, for another a *sāṛī*, for another some other requirements which arise from deep-seated unfulfilled wants, etc. This is not to analyse the reasons but to stress the fact that all words or signs or symbols are associated with images that in turn arise due to the past conditioning which is present in the very structure of the brain itself. This process of various associations is extremely rapid, beyond conscious human comprehension, and even beyond the most fantastic gadgets which man has made today. Thus, one can well imagine that in a normal conversation when hundreds of words are used to communicate, each one must be understanding the signals as they are received or transmitted in the context of thousands of images within the framework of one's own understanding. In other words, the communication which is sent out in one form, or with one motivation, is seldom received in the same form or structure by the recipient who superficially may continue to express his agreement or understandmg in the same manner without any verification. Messages are not really conveyed in their essence except rarely when total attention is being paid at that moment by those who are present at this exchange (*fig*. 5.1).

To state it still more simply, it is commonly believed that all the sense organs (especially the eyes and the ears and the other sense perceptions), receive the external world directly and clearly. It is well known for example that neither the eye as an organ nor the ear as an organ, see or hear something directly. But it is the signals received through these organs that are instantly interpreted or conceptualized in the brain which is already programmed at a certain level; for, whatever is received is understood in conformity with that conditioning or the experiential structure of the brain. This is why even in everyday life (at the very simple levels of communication outwardly) one might believe that what has been said is conveyed. Yet, we all know how even simple orders of action are seldom followed, and have therefore to be repeatedly stated in terms of various meanings, if no misinterpretation is to take place. One finds that, despite so many refinements in the language, or of rules and regulations, the simple tasks whether in organizations or even in relationships at the family level are seldom expressed or carried out. A great deal of misunderstanding of a trivial nature at the personal level and at larger levels is today common in the world. And so in the context of learning and communication it is this constant interpretation at the conceptual levels to which the entire system is so tied down. For instance, if one is specialized in one field, say botany or history at the academic level (or even specialized in the social task one performs in any profession), then whenever an event takes place it is viewed by all these different categories of people who believe these to be their identities. Thus the same event has as many interpretations as the number of people involved in different categories. Of course, each one might say that his eyes and ears are directly seeing and hearing the event in its actuality. Even the simple task of looking at the tree by different individuals, and their receptivity to that tree, is completely governed by their intellectual understanding or emotional state. As we know from our own lives, when we see a natural phenomenon it appears at one moment quite wonderful, at another quite ugly and yet at third time the mind is so absorbed in something else that it simply does not exist.

It is the state of mind which changes constantly from moment to moment and interprets and determines the receptivity of the external world as it is received via the sense organs. In this kind of conditioning, the brain is itself a large and amazing sense organ. It is conditioned because of the past evolutionary, racial, sociocultural background of thousands of years expressed in one individual's life. In this way, each individual is encased in his own universe. Sometimes in this encasement of concepts or images there is a break, or the lifting of the veils of appearance when the direct perception of reality takes place. Communication is successful at moments when there is the heightened intensity and especially so when one is viewing oceans, mountains, trees, flowers, rivers, waterfalls, birds in flights and so on. Sometimes this happens when the mind is miraculously open, listening and seeing creation with childlike wonder, or when two individuals communicate with each other for a fraction of a second without any preconceived notions. It is when we pay full attention to each other that the essence of what is being stated in so many ways gets across completely. As these moments one has experienced, and yet may not express it by these other words, that one intuitively knows, or truly understands another person completely. These moments which are for most part of our lives somehow brought about without any effort — often accidentally or out of the blue these seem so complete, so full, that they add up to a tremendous joy and often an ecstatic experience of the full feeling of, and for life. It is as if what is being said, and what is being received gives one an intuitive understanding of the essence of life. Life is not bound to the concepts of time and space. The experience referred to is eternal, or "out of time". This experience, often degraded to some kind of mysterious or irrational dimension, is an ignorance of the mystical though this label also seems to have nowadays become a derogatory one. But without it both learning and communication, of living "life" itself, gives one a sense of futility and meaninglessness, the widespread feeling of alienation. This is what has brought about immense misery, suffering and an alarming crisis in the human civilization of the day.

Barriers to Learning and Communication

It may be clear from what has been stated above about learning and communication that these are not separate or divergent, but closely interlinked processes. In order to learn and communicate deeply, one has to discard or keep in abeyance the knowledge accumulated in the psychological sense; of course not the information that one has to have for the day-to-day living. First, one has got to be conscious of barriers such as these. The discarding is to be of those identifications that somehow become part of one's psychological identity. It is this "identity" or attachment to the categories of thought (in terms of name and form associated both externally with various objects, or with ideas or notions) that are mere abstractions of actual experience or direct perception, and then only a few of the attributes are selected to form the psychological make-up of the individual called a "person". Most of this identity that "one becomes" takes place unconsciously, and within the social system, from the time of birth onwards. Later, it is reinforced in a self-conscious manner, by confirming to various individuals or social groups that one associates with during the different phases of one's life. This is a conditioning by either a kind of conformity to society's norms or even of revolting against such authority; both are part of the same process which govern a person's identity and his life. It is as if the entire life of the person is constantly seeking approval or attention from various groups or trying to fall in line with the ideas he has come to form of them. It is as if there were actually something realistic about such identity, with notions, ideas; and, ideals begin to act as a kind of authority, a separate entity.

With only a little attention given to these sundry aspects of being, what becomes apparent is that the social and cultural process in which the individual matures, midwifes an illusory (albeit real) form of a person — someone who plays a role in society. At every moment, each one plays a different role all the time, viz. as father, as son, as husband, as brother, or as a professional, depending on circumstances. Of course, this is how from times immemorial society has used various mechanisms to regulate the behaviour of individuals within the system so that it gives the maximum benefits for a smooth functioning. Ideally speaking, if each one played his or her role appropriately at all times there would be the smooth functioning of society. These various roles constitute an individual.

At the social level those several external and internal factors which bring about changes require a constant readjustment and appropriate behaviour from respective sections in order that a working balance takes place, both in the individual and in society at large. But imbalances are created when one or more subsystems change without proportionate change in the other subsystems; for instance, when norms break down, and when there are movements of people from one region to another and so on. Aspects of interpersonal behaviour, of kinship systems or of other life situations do not catch up in a very conscious manner with this sudden change in the system. Since situations of conflict and tension create disorder, upholders of society's norms and ideals, those who foresee and grasp the social process, may well create new norms and ideals as will perhaps bring about a harmonious balance for the malfunctioning system.

However, we know that imbalances create great disparities whether at the political, economic or social level although the three are actually closely interlinked. Often different subsystems see these changes as threats to their survival or the survival of the idea which has so far allowed it to somehow continue for a considerable period of time. In these subsystems or in the larger systems, the upholders of the norms and ideals (or those who are in power), become the defenders or protectors of the outmoded rules and regulations — politically or religiously they represent the orthodox elements. The preservation of power becomes the primary goal of survival, which is quite other than the attainment of a total or holistic view of the survival of the larger system, beyond one's sectional interests. As a consequence, the orthodoxy sees various imaginary or real threats from other quarters including one's own younger generation, which, because it has an open mind, easily adjusts or changes its pattern according to the new innovations or inventions that seep in through various means into the system. There is mobilization of all groups of people into the kind of polarity that now begins to emerge so that it is no longer a question of the maintenance of balance and harmony or of the "ideals" of human life, but human values become totally identified with those norms or abstract values to which individuals or groups strongly adhere. This is so because of the fear of either giving up its imaginary power or of adjusting and learning to, and from new situations, i.e. giving up compulsive conformity to custodian life — somehow believed to be the one and only way of defining a "balanced" existence.

Without going into the details of processes historically, those have been mentioned elsewhere (Malik 1977a, b), it should be clear that one aspect of the human mind is that caught up at the superficial level of the thought processes, structured in the unconscious, it may well become unwilling to discard outmoded ways of existence even if these are infructuous — obviously so. There is a close linkage of each individual, or each group's psychological identity with abstract ideals, so that even human lives are expendable at the expense of abstract ideas, and notions have to be upheld at all cost. Obviously, learning is at a standstill here. Now, whether one gives to this behaviour an orthodox, a conservative or any other label, the driving force behind it is that of preservation and it seems to smother the full expression of life. It is as if the humankind, as expressed in the social and cultural system, is willing to forego the true joy which is related to the quality of one's being. In this so-called living, attempts are made to influence behaviour by means of technological devices and with which we are rather familiar. All these sophisticated technological attempts are in fact endeavours arising from a deeper level of the human psyche, to be in touch with the essence, to be in "communion" once again with the core quality or qualities. But in these totally misdirected attempts, all that happens is that there is an increase of information, available very rapidly and very amply for different individuals. Yet, it is far removed from any intrinsic knowledge, that quality of being — an urge which is experienced at rare moments by all individuals. So, the quality of communication and learning will not change in the normal course of life, unless there is an awareness of the sociocultural conditioning that acts as a barrier to true learning or true communication.

Apparently quantity — it is generally assumed — will at some point of time metamorphose to quality. This is totally an erroneous notion, for quantity neither can bring about fundamental change, nor transformation in any society or in the life of an individual, since it is the accumulation of "the more of the same thing" in different garbs. Given this attitude and human perception, the so-called "developments" in terms of progress in the world, and which continue to increase by leaps and bounds, equally increase the frustration of the individual and of groups of whatever size, nations or multinational organizations. Even if "solved", the dimension of the crisis continues to exist at one place or the other and in one form or other despite the availability of enormous funds, personnel, intellect and so on.

The fact that no one is willing to discard or take the first step in unlearning, or giving up that which is not appropriate, it amounts to rigidity, the inability to relearn. The situation does not allow the essence, or the large context within which communication ought to take place, to materialize. Thus the "blind" continue to lead the blind, and very unself-consciously so, believing as if theirs were wide-awake, conscious efforts. It is like wearing dark glasses not knowing that one is wearing dark glasses, and yet continuing in various ways to clear the darkness outside by enormous effort without realizing that the obscurity itself is because of the glasses, having nothing to do with the external world. Obviously, to see light or clarity, the simplest thing to do is to take the glasses off whereby everything gets clear in an instant. In other words, the meaning of true transformation is to wake up from those dogmas, belief systems and conclusions, which prevent one from seeing or hearing, i.e. allow the complete functioning of sense organs which by themselves do not do so at full alertness, since the mind itself is narrowed or shut down verily like a horse with blinkers, that is not allowed to see, or cannot see anything beyond its nose.

Beyond Barriers

While it is obvious that it is the mind where the correction is to take place, this is not the place for any discussion of the various theoretical perspectives of what the mind is about as has been stated by different philosophies. Whether these are true or not would only take us once again into a kind of trap, since it is the mind itself which gets caught down into its own sophisticated web. The attempt suggested here is more to make the instrument, the mind, be aware of itself, of transforming the ability of each individual to experience living in such a way that the situations one has been trying to change, or has been putting up with clear up in the process of life itself, i.e. through one's ability of general awareness or attention, without any preconceived notions, beliefs or conclusions. In fact a conclusion means that somehow life is concluded, i.e. if there are conclusions or beliefs about life then one lives life according to abstract notions, even ideals in the sense of a mechanical repetition rather a continuous openness of mind, which is to live from moment to moment. The light of self awareness and attention itself keeps clearing the path as one moves along and there is nothing to be done as such which one imagines if one moves without this light. This is called witnessing or choiceless awareness. In other words, for the most part our lives are today patterned in a structure which only allows for a philosophy or world view of winning or succeeding or appearing to others as if we are successful. The rules of this game have been in existence for centuries and are established in the culture at large. It includes all aspects of one's life, the very many complexes, guilts and relationships where every experience involves a concomitant judgement and conclusion in everyday life, i.e. this is good or this is bad, this is right and this is wrong or this is not worth much, in a competitive and comparative way.

Given such a situation no transformation can take place since we do not even have an awareness of what it is at stake. The prevailing conceptual reality therefore continues to determine what we think is real. It stops us from the creation of those other possibilities which are automatically deemed to be impossible. Thus, transformation takes place at two levels. One, in creating an environment which allows us for this kind of commitment, for a possibility of the impossible, a context of transformation rather than its denial. The other is for people to discover for themselves, or enable people to think for themselves, allowing the possibility for these kinds of transformation regardless of seeking approval and attention; in other words, to aim at being more than a mere "effect" of the environment, beyond causal notions, linear time, reasons and so on. The very first step is to allow the possibility of raising such questions which will radically reorganize the human problems and possibilities. This amounts to asking such question as "what have I believed to be true or is it an interpretation and even at that my interpretation? Do I believe what is believed to be true or do I live in the context of truth? Do I take a stand or commitment of my own life or those around me as a total responsibility or am I a victim of circumstances in which blame and guilt are the major belief systems about myself or the others?", and so on. It is crucial to raise these questions about the purpose of our lives, about the ways that are available to each one of us as a human being, and to think about the possibility of the future whereby "beingness" comes more naturally to people (Bartley 1978).

Questions such as these imply that the individual has to look within, in order to live face-to-face with himself, and in order that he may get the ability to live without ascribing meaning to situations where none exists. It means to live every moment with responsibility towards oneself and for everything around one. It can mean taking action founded not on abstractions but on the strength of one's word in the context of the quality of being, with which becoming happens, and not simply oriented to an "achievement and becoming" orientation. Thinking thus, an individual comes into an enormous responsibility for his own way of life, a kind of courage to live without ostensible reason or motivation, and to stand face-to-face with the perennial question "who am I?" This is the question of the being, the human, and which at first seems an enormous one, frightening, since it demands the letting go. The giving up of a faulty notion of the human personality, results in an expansiveness, the joy often referred to as "ecstatic bliss". This is beyond the available linguistic means of comprehension and expression.

6

The Person
Physical and Social Conditioning

FROM what has been stated in Chapter 5 about learning and communication, it will be clear that abstract ideas and notions often govern, nay even tyrannize behaviour. By and large most of such notions are manifested unconsciously since almost everybody is busy with the business of living. "Wilful consciousness" is a superficial level, but which is what we imagine to be the primary fact of our life. It is in truth a reaction to the unconscious depths of the mind. An appropriate analogy here may be the waves on the ocean, which are a result of many variables, such as several currents occurring in the depth of ocean, atmospheric conditions, the pull of gravity, the phases of the moon and so on. However, the wave itself may well "imagine", it has some wilful deliberate choice on its part in the way it functions. In the same way, a person imagines that his very existence, for a short duration, is due to his wilful choice. The appearance and disappearance of the bubble — the person — is in the context of waves and the ocean — an integral totality.

In the same way, there are many levels of accumulated experiences, both complete and incomplete, that form the unconscious layers — racial, biological, social, etc. — which exist within the mind. These hidden forms express themselves in many different ways at the superficial levels of what we call consciousness or self-consciousness of the person. One imagines, on the other hand, that the self-consciousness attributable to one's personality is a "real" entity, and thereby itself separate from the unfathomable depths. In separating personality from the larger whole of which not only is its part, but its very nature being that of whole, causes what has been called the illusion, an illusory self. The operational entity, which is what a person is, mistakenly takes itself to be a separate reality. Is this erroneous notion not one of the key causes of the immense misery and suffering of mankind?

The enormous suffering of the "individual" — person — is precisely because he or she takes himself or herself to be primarily a separate entity. This widespread attitude, at the level of the "stream of consciousness" in which mankind subsists, contributes in a way to the larger pool of the travails of each other in larger and larger groups. It is like when, with a stone thrown into a lake, the impact of the waves travels to the shores of the lake surface. If many such stones which cause agitation are dropped into the lake, these effect each other and spread all over the surface. In this metaphor even separate individuals both effect and are affected by other individuals since each one exists in that totality or wholeness of the water or the ocean. It is a total illusory notion that each individual has a separate consciousness of his own, unrelated to everything else. It is like the case of fish in water which perhaps are oblivious of the fact that they are all part of the water in which they exist. The individual, person, however is both unique and universal at the same time. In a way, while all snowflakes are alike, in their individual patterns no two snowflakes are alike. While every moment — as an event — is unique and not repeatable, it is universal as well. Its memory as mechanical thought — a commentary on the experience — makes it appear to have continuity by creating conceptual space–time coordinates.

At any rate, to recapitulate, we have been discussing the problem of learning and communication, in the total perspective within which exist levels of experience and its conceptualization. The latter is reflected in various forms and functions such as the structure of language, i.e. symbolically representing various ideas, images and views. This is how each individual or group receives the objects of the external world including his own name and form. At the operational level this categorization simplifies day-to-day activities, and is essential if daily life is to continue in some coordinated and patterned manner. In fact, the senses that perceive external objects may only be received in the mind in this manner since, to exaggerate, the actual dimensions of the external objects cannot certainly be put into the human brain. The storage and interpretation of the signals received from outside are necessarily to be coded into this very sophisticated and complicated computer. In terms of the human evolution and the evolution of the world, there is a close interaction of man and nature speaking from the viewpoint of differentiation — within the total unified field of a certain cosmic intelligence or energy. For the moment, and for the sake of argument, let us keep these two categories of the individual, person, and the receptivity of the external world as separate entities; as a kind of working hypothesis which perhaps is feasible and certainly widely prevalent in the modern world, in order thereby to seek the interrelationship and the conditioning of the individual at the gross physical and social cultural levels, both spatially and temporally.

Physical Conditioning

As said above, there is a false separation of the individual from society, nature and the surrounding cosmos because of various kinds of conceptualizations. In this section, however, we may simply take the entire human body and its master controller, the brain, as a sense organ for a discussion of the vast inter-relationships. This bodily instrument has emerged through long evolutionary pressures. In terms of contemporary knowledge, that is, from such sciences as physics, chemistry, biology and so on, it is clear that the physical body is made up of the same elements as the earth itself is. The nature of these elements is the same in all forms of matter that has been classified into living and non-living, organic and inorganic, for our own comprehension. From the viewpoint of the elementary particles and waves there are no such distinctions. Of course, elements combine in various permutations and combinations into simple or complex structures ranging from what we call "solid", say a rock, to the delicate constitution of the human body. But all this is a one continuous system without any separation whatsoever in actual fact. Conceptual differences created for operational purposes are mistaken for actual truth. This is one symptom of the crisis of civilization. From the viewpoint of ancient philosophies there is a simplified way of stating that all forms of matter are made up of five basic elements and their various combinations.

In whatever way we may explain the human system, it has certainly emerged from the elements of the earth which included its environment of course. A product of the earth may consider itself separate, yet it is a part and parcel of it. While we consider trees, stones and creatures to be an intrinsic part of nature, yet man either because of his technological ingenuity or because he can move about so rapidly, or because he is so hopelessly lost in the conceptual dimensions of his thoughts or the brain system, or that he can control and exploit nature or earth itself, it is as if he has forgotten his origins or links with the earth. He has alienated himself, through this ability of creating culture to believe his separation and unrelatedness to each and everything — not to mention the very cosmos itself, of which course he is an irrevocable part. It is ironical that man as an end result, as one of the attributes of earth, has also the capacity to destroying his own progenitor. At the moment we are not taking into account the quality called consciousness and which has a wider implication for the existence of matter itself — source from which man has separated himself to multiply anguish, alienation and helplessness.

The human body is taken to be the basis of the ego or the self as the individual unit. Normally, a person does identify himself with the body and treats himself to be an offspring of his or her parents. Even purely physiologically, leaving aside the potentialities that exist in the brain or mental states, from the minutest physical part to all the gross features, these are all genetically determined in terms of the combination of genetic DNA, RNA, etc. molecules which combine when the fertilization of the ovum takes place. The genetic material programmes the body of the person as he grows from this fertilized egg to a fully developed human form. He is completely determined by those genetic traits that are present in the parental body — the fertilized ovum. In this, there is absolutely no choice for a person who completely identifies himself with the bodily structure that has been given various names and labels or subsequently conditioned socioculturally. This fundamental fact cannot in any way be altered without causing harm to the bodily system even though everyone sometimes or the other wishes and desires to be different even physically than what he or she is. This wish may arise from some ideal notions, mythologies, and indeed even from television or cinema heroes or heroines, and other attempts to conform to sociocultural norms. The bodily system, including the fact of being a male or female, is already determined and there is no choice whatsoever, if any, to be different so to speak from this "solid" fact.

The functioning of each part of the bodily system, apart from little deviations or adaptations (because of the overall environment), is also programmed. The body's duration and of its subsystems stop functioning when there is a signal from the genetic material to come to an end in one manner or the other. Humankind may attempt to prolong this duration from the time of fertilization to actual birth into the outer world, through childhood, youth, middle and old age. But the death of the bodily system is determined irrevocably. Yet, somehow in the conceptual or dream world that man lives in he somehow, much too often, forgets the fundamental nature of the existence of the purely physical system despite the amazing fact of his or her viewing other individuals or persons as well as plants and animals which clearly seem to undergo these developmental stages of a life history and death of organisms. This matter is brought home so clearly in close relationships, and the impact is not much when there is the news of the coming and going of so many distant human beings with whom there is no personal relationship. But such a deep impact is somehow either blocked or other avenues of escape are found which make one forget that the person's own bodily system is governed and determined by the same laws as are applicable to the world and nature all around. At the moment, one need not digress into this paradoxical situation of birth and death, that one normally tends to ignore.

Genetic inheritance obviously is not limited to one's parents since they are also the outcome of the same inheritable genetic material, for which they had no choice either. The coming together of two people in bringing about a new birth is also determined according to the intrinsic functioning laid down by the genetic material. Parents seldom consciously determine either the sex or nature of the offspring. This is at the simplified level ignoring all the multiple factors that go into the process. The parents' existence is determined in the same manner by their parents and further by the parents' parents and so on of which there are countless generations. The genetic material is a coded symbolic representation of the chemical material for all kinds of forms and their functioning in the purely physical or biological world that we visualize all around us. Thus, there exists within one individual a long chain of genetic material. But, who for most parts identifies herself or himself closely with the immediate parents or relatives of that generation or perhaps with the near ancestors wherever such genealogical charts are available, does it in terms of sociocultural norms rather than purely from the point of view of genetic material.

From the evolutionary genetic viewpoint what is present in the person or individual — in one, in "me" — is a continuous product of generations which go back to the earliest human forms. If we continue to visualize these processes even further, then it is imperative to take into account the entire primate evolution from which man has arisen and is an intricate part of the same system. The primate system then assumes a subsystem of the other mammalian systems or further back to reptilian subsystems; all of which are subsystems within, to simplify it further, the other forms of plant and animal life or even the tiniest, what we label as elementary animate forms existing in the oceanic depths, or the earliest phases. By this logic, if we stretch it back even further our hypothetical separation of organic evolution from the inorganic also disappears. Ultimately, the fundamental stuff or "material" are elementary particles or waves, and in both the organic or inorganic are the same.

In other words, the entire inorganic forms of matter are an essential basis for the evolution of the organic forms in which the genetic material is coded. It is this entire evolution present in each person, beginning from the basic elements that we call inanimate to the animate and to highly developed animal forms leading to man and to the specific person. In this individual the entire ontological and phylogenetic evolution certainly determines its existence. Moreover, it is present in him — in the Now — in order for him to function in that form completely and totally. For biologists it is well known that in the womb the embryo rapidly recapitulates all the earlier forms of evolution in the embryonic stage; as if evolution recreates itself through every creature. While it repeats itself conceptually speaking, yet it is unique in each and every moment of creation and destruction.

We may even continue to see this process further since the primary form of matter is the earth itself with all its elements, so that the entire earth is almost as if present in that, in the specific individual completely and totally. It is not only in terms of elementary matter that we have mentioned but even in the evolutionary sense that a "historic" record is present in that total brain–body system. And one may ask, what is it that impinges upon the earth to function and move the way it does? Because the way it moves and functions in the solar system is intricately tied to its satellite, the moon, the other planets and most of all the sun, which is at the centre of our solar system. Every planet and its satellites including the functioning of the sun closely determine what happens to the earth — and what happens to us on the earth — which includes the atmosphere, the oceans and the land form. It is well known that even a slight deviation of the moon's functioning and its relationships to earth or a fraction of disturbance on the sun, and similarly elsewhere, upsets the planets and may transform the existing state of affairs on earth — so much so that the mere flash of a disturbance from without or within the deepest recesses of the earth may cause the microscopic and its man–animal or planet relations to disappear without a trace. Such is the precarious balance of the earth and its inhabitants, much as it is part of the entire solar system.

The solar system, which we take to be the system within which earth functions, is therefore also carefully patterned and yet it once again becomes a subsystem of the many other subsystems that exist within — there are many millions within what is called the Milky Way galaxy. In turn, the galaxy becomes a subsystem of the billions of other galaxies we know of and so on.

The point in this very simplified picture is to show that in the human individual there is a backing of the entire universe both in its form and functioning. Just as a geologist can read the entire history of the earth in a rock, similarly the universe is present in this bodily system, especially if it is to function fully and completely. The human system is therefore just like, "it were the earth" like the universe itself, being continuously related to myriad forms as an ongoing process. The universe is both within and without, speaking in dualities, owing to limitations of language, because in actuality there is no within and without of the unlimited system that we call the universe.

Apart from the evolutionary perspective, there are spatial interrelationships, i.e. the environment moving along with the earth's gravity even as the earth rotates. To this the individual bodily system is closely interrelated even spatially, i.e. to the ground that he stands on, or whatever structure he may have built for himself. There is contiguity and continuity; he is part and parcel of those other beings that exist on the same terrestrial area, including the atmosphere. The various divisions into this or that, or other boundaries, of longitude or latitude that have been devised, are for operational purposes. While there may be ecological zones, all these merge into each other since the earth is one unit. It is like one large carpet on which there are individuals standing, yet the ground is the same for all individuals, being connected through that "carpet" which we may call the earth, to breathe the same common air. Similarly, all the other sundry activities are within one and same framework and the same "ground of being". Spatially, the earth is then similarly linked to other planetary and solar systems and so on. This framework of evolution or time and space interrelationship brings forth the fact of a one continuous movement. That is, whatever happens at the microscopic level, this happening takes place at the macroscopic level too. This is so because everything at all levels takes place everywhere, vis-à-vis everything else. Nothing is in isolation, for anything to happen everything is responsible. Conversely, not only does the universe influence the behaviour of the individual to function the way it does, in a universal–spherical system, every point becomes the centre — its functioning depending upon the given point of view. The so-called tiny particle, of the little individual in this way (who in the twentieth century considers himself to be of little significance) assumes the same power as the universe itself — in him exist the same powers and dimensions which can move, change or transform the rest of the universe. In other words, the little drop is also the ocean, contributing to the making of that ocean with equal significance. "I am the universe and the universe is me." This is Indira's web or the universe is a holograph (Morrison 1982).

This brief exposition will help us understand what we mean by the individual self and its ability to transform the universe by a simple transformation of his or her perspective. The enormity of the power behind the universe in the individual has been totally overlooked in the darkness of the current state of knowledge which we have said is the ignorance of the essential nature of man.

Social Conditioning

In terms of sheer physical matter, the close linkage of the body with nature, environment, the earth and the universe both in the evolutionary sense and spatially was briefly noted above. One might say that the behavioural pattern of the physiological organism is totally conditioned or limited by its own make-up, such as sense organs and all the other parts which have built-in codes of conduct. This conditioning would cover both the instinctive response, as well as learned behaviour.

The brain is also a supersensory organ in which are coded messages (neurons, etc.), very intricately regulating stimulus–response behavioural patterns and so on. The creation of coded symbols in the form of language, ideas and images is part of the sociocultural pattern within which one is brought up. This controls one's behaviour through the body. There is no separation between the body and the brain, for they function together as a psychosomatic operational apparatus, where various permutations and combinations take place. Individual and group thinking plays a significant role in the various processes and patterns that govern the behaviour of human societies. But, by and large, the impression is that because a great choice is available to the individual or a group whereby one can decide or choose options for one's behaviour that there is a freedom of choice. It is thought that there is some will or deliberate choice as opposed to the conditioned behaviour of bodily functions which are already given. But this fundamental premise has to be re-examined very carefully in terms of sociocultural conditioning.

Without going into the nature of the fertilized ovum (and into what constitutes consciousness, or the available predetermined potentialities that exist in the specific newly formed individual), from the moment of coming into the outside world the human baby is governed by the sociocultural environment. The immediate influence is that of the parents who themselves are governed by the matrix of this cultural environment, belief systems, kinship systems, mythologies and all the other paraphernalia of cultural and socialized behaviour in every detail within which they function almost as if it were a natural behaviour. This is instinctive in the sense that every other human group expresses the same basic needs and desires in many ways. Thus, the infant's socialization is determined, not only by the genetic material and its potentialities, the racial memories, but also what we commonly define as those "sociocultural" traditions that have been handed down generation after generation, centuries upon centuries.

If we carefully pay attention to this process (whatever the explanation by way of various cultural concepts and models for the origin and accumulated knowledge existing from times immemorial in various combinations), the same determinant continues to be present in the cultural matrix in which contemporary society exists at one level of development or the other. This entire knowledge operates in the present "existential moment" in much the same way as the physiological body is both a result and a determinant of the entire universal process. A very simple example in technology and its cultural expression would be the invention of fire which once made, continues to be handed down until today, even if in a greatly modified form. Or, the other various ways that energy has been harnessed continues to exist or becomes a foundation of other forms of energy, both in purely technical terms or in terms of social groups. Similarly, many other forms of habit or habitat, ways of sitting, interpersonal behaviour and food habits are all based on foundations which go into the dim antiquity of such traditions handed down generation after generation, the world over.

In the process it is the storage of knowledge in a generalized, what we may call memory pool, which operates or expresses itself in the human individual or through various institutionalized cultural forms in every human society. This is what allows for a continuity in traditions. We are not making a great distinction between higher forms of tradition, or the lower, since that is a matter of professional debate. But a generalized mechanism of the kind is applicable in all spheres, and is easily understandable. Traditions are conceptualized and coded variously by images, the structure of language rites and rituals, in music and dance or other arts, economic transactions and so on; areas which are all intertwined in the ongoing life of a giving human society.

Accordingly, the human infant receiving many varied kinds of communication and learning from his environment and most of all from his parents and especially the mother, starts to record in terms of his own potentialities available within the complex genetic material, the images being sent out for his personality formation. To emphasize once again, words are not what matter, since the infant is very sensitive, his sense organs are open to every nuance and variation and feeling and mood of what is being conveyed to him directly and indirectly. The brain is receiving signals at all times especially more so at the infant stage. This is true even at the adult stage (although the latter is so caught up in his "conscious" self that he is unaware that a narrow vision has blocked the total functioning of the brain) both in terms of receiving and sending out signals.

It is common knowledge that even if two people are talking to each other the brain itself registers all sensory signals somehow by itself, especially if there is a danger to the physiological organism. One may imagine how alert and open the sensory organs of the infant must be. It is well-known to psychologists that not only is the same true for the infant but that even already in the womb the child is sensitively receiving signals from what is going on outside. It has been noted that if a remark is made "you are very ugly" the deeper implications of this are immediately communicated to the child. Several such communications to it (or between parents who for example may be quarrelling in another room) are immediately conveyed to the psychosomatic set-up of the young individual. These kinds of recordings become the foundation like a geometrical progression of data, received in terms of feelings and emotions. This results in the kind of behaviour expected, responses which the brain soon learns as a survival mechanism for both its physiological and social good. A kind of mechanism of expectations and demands within which parents and society themselves function begins to operate in the infant.

The abstract ideological expectations and demands arise from the notion of attention and approval, reward and punishment, "you vs me", etc. It is one framework within which most personalities function and the infant does the same. In a society governed by many negative notions a great deal of attention is given to pain and misery, or disease-orientation rather than health-orientation; in other words, all the dual binary oppositions which we have mentioned elsewhere. When the infant is satisfied and left alone he discovers for instance that hardly any attention is given to it, and that he is somehow left alone: without human contact. If this be the case, the human brain is discovering and learning wonderful marvels from an extraordinary world; and infants and children are constantly experimenting to discovering new things, both in terms of fun and survival. At the level of approval-and-attention this infant for some genuine or other reason starts to cry or gives a big shout to which the response of one or both the parents is to come running, provide it immediate comfort or relieve it through some kind of contact or by providing pleasure. This amounts to a great discovery for the infant. As most grownups in the modern world know that to any shout in distress or any other kind of "screaming-help" which sounds very urgent, immediate attention tends to be given. At any rate, since the whole social matrix is one of an attention-approval game in a kind of insecure state in this psychological matrix, the infant quickly learns. He, therefore, bases his own behaviour on this dominating pattern that continues throughout his childhood in educational and other cultural institutions. Pain and crisis situations become a norm for social and individual functioning. This is a conditioning of the brain which is constantly creating crisis situations: it is in fact an addiction, the biggest of them all!

The individual is therefore conditioned to behave in a certain manner even if the choices available seem to be several. Sociocultural behaviour is, thus, a conditioned response. This conditioning is coded most commonly at the level of thought which covers all spheres of activity. So whenever in any relationship there is a verbal statement expressing any form of communication, there is a set response from the receiver as well. As illustrated earlier, if a certain word is conveyed it immediately elicits, through thought association, various responses without any wilful choice at the instant from the individual. This is part of that stimulus–response mechanism that creates a whole series of images which stir up both surface and deeper unconscious hidden meanings within each individual and the group's psychological make-up. One may imagine what happens when a series of sentences are continuously being spoken and addressed to each other, how rapidly and instantly the complicated computer must quickly record, search into its own memory banks and respond almost as if it has understood. At the gross level this is the framework in our normal life.

In other words, it is a conditioned response of all the

socialization in the cultural institutions within which we live. This kind of functioning operates at all levels, of feelings, emotions and what we call conscious levels of thought or superficial thinking which each one believes as if to be a conscious choice. To take another example, we like or dislike another person at first sight. It is conditioned by our response based on the previous data, such as, if there is an association of a bad experience with someone wearing a red shirt as has been recorded in the memory pool, there is an instant recall of the previous experience, and to the surface of the mind appears a response instantly without going into reason of it that one does not "like" this individual somehow. One is not conscious of how associations of feelings and emotions recorded from infancy, etc. produce this response so that one tends to have what one refers an instinctive response, of feeling "I do not like him". One can imagine the responses that work in a much more complicated way in the brain which receives the signals from the outer world at so many levels and are sorted out in the computer which contains data that is governed by many ideas, images and dream worlds that are constantly being cleared up in the brain.

Whatever the explanation, these are all conditioned responses of our likes and dislikes, pleasures and pains within what we may call a psychosocial complex called the "personality". What we believe to be our conscious level of thinking is the surface layer of the unconscious depths of our psyche which govern the behaviour patterns and is not in our control, at least immediately. It is common knowledge that this kind of thinking, call it brain "chatter" goes on perpetually during hours of wakefulness or at the level of dreams in some form or the other. What we call "my own thinking" is a simplistic notion since it is not in one's control to start or stop this. Anyone may be asked to start or stop it and he will be hard put to do so although each one of us claims that this is "my thinking". It is clear that not only is the body but our behavioural patterns and expressions of it within the structure of language, ideas and images in whatever form are also conditioned and operated unconsciously or automatically.

To sum up, we thus come to that stage where we know that

both contemporary and the earlier development of thousands of years at both the physical level of matter and its associated sociocultural dimensions of equal antiquity have produced entities which we label as the human species. It has, by and large, behaved unconsciously and totally conditioned. Most of the brain, as the main organ, is totally conditioned and it has become addicted to the stimulus–response behaviour of the coded symbols with all the implications and depths at the ideational or imaginary level rather than with the actual and direct response to any fact of sensory perceptions. Given this state of affairs, there is little wonder that man and civilization are in a state of crisis since all attempts to rectify or transform are, or have become, make-believe unconscious actions, or shall we say non-action? What then is action? Given this situation, does the person have a will? Or, is the person, the thinker, a mere movement of thought? If so, what happens to the experiential self?

7

The Person
Will and Loss of Experience

Does the Person Have a Will?

WITHOUT going into the semantics of the "person", the word person, as said earlier, the "I" is identifiable — in one of the meanings of the term — with the physical body. This socio-physical and psychosomatic complex is the result of a series of evolutionary stages as well as the interrelationship in its living behavioural existence to all of the rest of mankind and the natural enviornment. It is determined both temporally and spatially, that is, it is conditioned to act the way it does because of all of the factors involved, and in which it has little choice. Similarly at the mental level or in terms of functioning of the brain, behavioural patterns of this person or individual which cognizes body and identifies with it, is socioculturally determined as well. The person brought up in that matrix is also conditioned without much choice. One might dispute it to say that there are various possibilities with the choices available within which each person believes he is taking a decision, as if he chooses or decides. But the availability of various choices and possibilities, however large the number may appear, is still the limitation of the choice that is available to this physio-socio-psychological entity (*fig*. 7.1).

If, for instance, we take the case — perhaps of a rock — we can say that choices for it are limited since it can either stay put, where it is or be pushed by an external force in order to move.

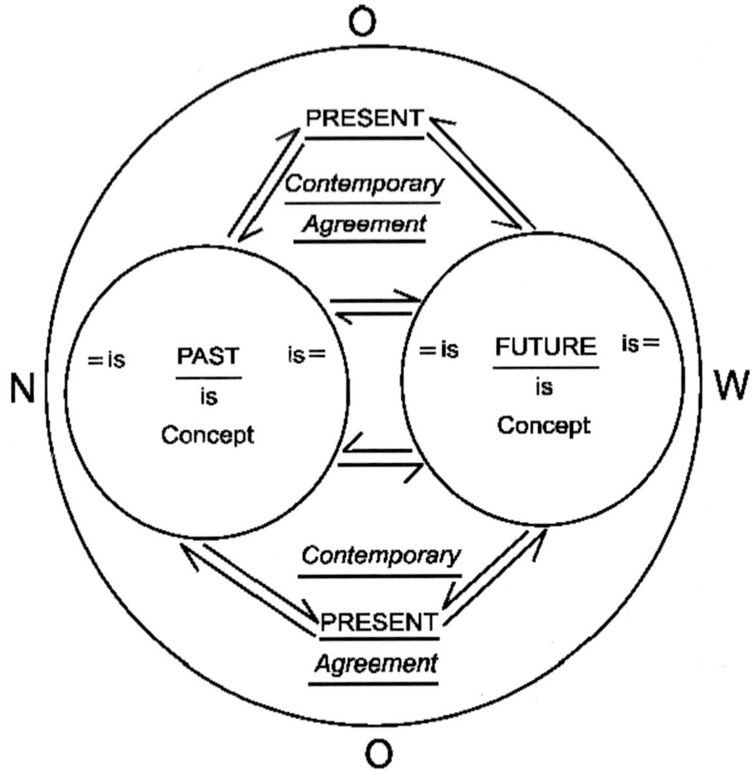

fig.7.1: Content is concept

Explanation to *fig*. 7.1

The person is a concept as said earlier, located in words, thoughts, language categorized like that, and IT function together with body as the basis, or together go name and form. All this is seen has reality in this way that one is conditioned in and by society. Yet it feels as if it is all actual and real, being mesmerized and hypnotized from or before one–this psychosomatic structure is brought into the world. If one contemplates and examines this socio-cultural existence, investigates it then some clarity may arise. This is important because layers or veils that cover the fundamental nature, the falseness of the entire structure begins to reveal itself even though it is like peeling an onion when practically nothing is left perhaps a tiny seed. This is shocking at first, and there are moments when this so-called emptiness is felt, where there are no thoughts, there is no movement, there is no chatter in the head, the constant commentary of the "little professor" as Gurdieff calls it.

The structure of linear time is a concept, reality is a social agreement only depending on the cultural context. Even the phenomenal world is a concept, i.e. once the earth is flat, the earth was the centre of the world and the sun rotates around it and so on. That is indeed a changing conceptual world, a mental projection for the individual and collective, contemporary as the present world, and at present is defined in this linear timescale from what refers to as the past, made up individual and collective memories which are indeed interpretations accepted by dominant groups. Historical narratives are also imaginary and fictional, collectively and individually. It keeps changing given the context and situation. There are many narratives, all notional and emotional.

All this comes under the notion of an "as if" world. The future is a projection from the past to the present and to the future. The future is projection from the past, it is not independent existence, it is all one continuum, there is no entity as the past, present or future. All this is imagined and occurs within the moments of NOW, the context of contents, and the contents are imagined within this empty space, void or all-pervasive energy. It is like what is written is important, the words, letters and sentences on the empty space, the white sheet, but one seldom gives attention to that, the context within which everything content, in fact, concepts take place exist.

The content of the universe is also sparse and meagre, just like the human or other bodies consist mainly of empty space, water and it is all moving, changing, breaking down and creating new forms within that vast mass of energy. However, within linguistic structure makes one appears as "solid"–words give it solidity and form. The word is the form, the object the thing. If one does not label and name phenomenon it does not exist. Words create the world as separate fragmented categories. No words, no language, it is all one continuum. We are told it is in that belief system of separateness by creating categories apparently for logical statements but one soon forgets that these statements are not actual. The map is only a hypothetical statement of the actual. The city in a map is nothing like experiencing the same actual city!!

In the case of an early form of living matter, say that of a frog, we are able to pinpoint the number of choices available because of the system it is functioning within and therefore are able to say that it has no choice even if the possibilities are now much more than is the case for the rock. We may move to an even more complicated living system such as when we notice that the number of choices increases considerably within which conditioning the animal can operate in a far sophisticated manner than is the case with the rock with which we began. When we come to our own mechanism it is the same conditioning, albeit the matter is much more complicated both in the physical nature of the body–brain structure as well as the cultural matrix within which this entity operates. Moreover, with the psychological make-up it is almost impossible to comprehend it especially on one's own. It is in this given structure that we believe each one of us is wilfully exerting a choice. We believe as if it is an open system of choices, or "I" have a "free will".

Giving attention by a kind of choiceless awareness, it is self-evident that the area of interaction and behaviour of this physio-socio-psychological complex is limited and conditioned in terms of the availability of choices. It is like walking along a road when there is no choice except for one to take a zig-zag movement, or follow in another pattern albeit moving in the same direction as the road. In this way, all kinds of deviations are possible, and that may be perhaps the only way we may say that there is a choice of behaviour. Nevertheless, it is still governed by the limitations of the road and the path already available including the direction of movement, governed by one's physically-given mechanism or the given experiential structure. Perhaps, compared to other inanimate and animate species, there is a flexibility of some kind which allows us to say that a person can determine or a society can determine or humankind can determine its own destiny. At the level from which we are talking about there is no choice available, unless there is that kind of awareness or consciousness which is rarely used by humankind. Yet, the first step is to be aware of this conditioning, if it is to be brought into focus, i.e. to make the person or individual aware of these limitations which become the unconscious controlling factors in one's behaviour. But without this kind of attention and awareness, being unconscious of these fundamental dimensions, the so-called self-consciousness of this entity called the person is completely determined or conditioned without any possibility of the application of a free will or choice, that is so often imagined to be operating.

The "person" at this level becomes a mere pawn or operational entity within the framework of hidden concepts of not only the social environment but the biological ones as well. His role is already determined by the genetic material which at the time of birth makes it into a female or male form whose psychosocial status is also determined in that specific culture. Thus, if one is a man or a woman the kind of behaviour expected and the ideals and norms of behaviour are already handed to him or her within the prevalent or existing traditions. Thus, apart from the potentialities which already exist in a physiological manner within, the mechanism is limited to experience that complexity, which is now identified with being a male or a female. Apart from the determinants within the social milieu the response of the physical mechanism is itself imbibed with that quality of maleness or femaleness, that is, the response to the external world is already built in from the viewpoint that is stored within the brain from times immemorial. Every experience of a female or a woman, even the physical stimulus or environment, is closely interlinked with the upbringing. It is a totally different experience almost unknowable to the male of the species who responds to the environment because of his predisposition to the qualities of maleness. Thus, the man's experience of the world and his response to a woman are because of his qualities of maleness whereby he knows the femaleness of another. But he cannot in the normal sense of the word ever experience himself or herself — as the case may be — the experience of being or having the qualities of maleness or femaleness of the other. The identification of this personality complex at the mere physical level with these limited aggregate of sense perceptions and functions is its limitation. On top of that, various other ideas in the social upbringing govern the behaviour pattern.

One might say that this conditioning therefore does not allow for much change in man's control over his own future or destiny. For example, the role of women is given a second place in a male-dominated society. But sociocultural change through economics and politics has brought about a great deal of fundamental changes in the role of women in modern societies. This does not detract us from the basic notion that there is flexibility of choice, of possibilities of change and continuity. Yet this is clearly determined in the sense that the viewpoint is still one of maleness and femaleness or their balance psychologically, culturally or even within the organism which governs the behavioural patterns of human beings. The conceptual framework continues to be one of confrontation. Perhaps it can be transformed to one of cooperation depending upon which world view and metaphysics one is governed by. But at the level of manifestation the name and form and simple categorization into two sexes is the structure within which human societies function, i.e. the person operates within the limited boundaries of that system.

So strong is this notion and identity that it would psychologically be called the ego, being a set of various attributes which have been put together in terms of expectations and demands or other ideals and norms. Or, the choice is made because of the factors of pleasure and pain, or comfort and discomfort, and so on that together give rise to what is called "I". This "I" plays various roles relative to the "other" within the social system and continuously does so all of the time without any choice. It is so ingrained and conditioned that the actual existence of this person or "I" becomes an enduring entity, which somehow seems to be eternal in nature, i.e. the person and the society he lives in begin to believe in their separate existence. The lack of awareness of this conditioning is one of the factors of the belief in a separate entity, with the choice of free will and independence.

At the level of the personality there is in fact no free will or freedom whatsoever although in common general behaviour the limited choices within which one can operate and choose make one believe that there is freedom of choice. Just like there is no choice for man to fly like birds with wings, so also is psychosocial behaviour limited to that conditioning and the make-believe notion of being a separate entity. This separate identity — howsoever wide ranging in its spectrum — stays limited and therefore views the world from those particular spectacles only, i.e. whatever the colour of the glasses he or she is wearing determines the knowledge of the external world to that extent only. With increasing sophistication the ego game becomes subtle which is constantly adapting and adopting new formulations in order somehow to maintain its own existence. It is, as is commonly said, the rope is tied to the peg of the ego, and howsoever long this rope may be its movement is still determined in all directions as far as one can go, by this peg, even if it sometimes appears to be lost from sight.

There is the parable of some people sitting in a boat at night who continue to row all night thinking they have crossed the river. But they find in the morning that they have not moved one inch because the boat was tied to the pole all the time. The predicament of the personality is just the same even in its false notion of denying its entity it attempts to free itself; and, this attempt itself further strengthens the personality and allows for its continuity ad nauseam. All these attempts arise because of the faulty notion of a separate entity whose true nature is blocked out, and this itself causes insecurity and uncertainty. For deep within the innermost recesses of consciousness is the knowledge that this entity is non-existent and an illusion. This is the fear and anxiety that man is constantly facing in his existence of not knowing his true self apart from all other factors that the superficial level only reinforces the notion of gaining freedom and security by various means.

That entity which seeks this freedom and security continues to live in the same fear and anxiety because, can a false entity possibly find security? That which is an insecure and an ephemeral entity cannot possibly either know the eternal or become the eternal. That which has no true existence, cannot know what existence is. That which is finite cannot know the infinite. It is like measuring the ocean with a small bucket; for not only is the measure small that it can never measure the immeasurable, but like the personality which the bucket is, it has even a hole in its bottom, so that nothing is retained in it. The personality is of this nature which in its illusion continuously perpetuates itself, as if attempting to fill the bucket hoping to measure the infinite. Primarily an awareness of bondage is necessary to be free. But in that very awareness there is the discovery that there is no bondage!

Thus, the view of the world based on this conditioned entity with the focus on the body and its accompanied socio-psychological make-up is only a viewpoint, and that too a very limited one within which framework one hopes, totally mistakenly, to obtain truth and knowledge. Until we inquire deeply into this unit we cannot count beyond. The search, if one sees this false notion, is to be aware that the unit which seeks is what is the sought, i.e. the seeker is the sought. Within the depths of one's consciousness this truth hides and wants to surface for there is not even the division of the external or internal world. The kind of acute "internal" awareness has to be brought back into focus. It is a breaking away from this somehow eternal identification of the body with the mental structure and the memories incorporated in it, if it is to become actual. While the person is all of this, that which knows has a body, has a mental complex, it has memories and so on; it has all this, but it is not one of these things. The knower is beyond, it is within, and much beyond it all. It is the unknown, nameless and formless.

The Loss of Experience

We have been talking about the person or the self as a physical, psychological and social complexity, i.e. an entity within the framework or focus of the form of what we label as the human body. It has been stated that this is a conditioned entity determined by innumerable variables both in terms of the "internal" and "external" factors. The mental make-up consists of a record of innumerable experiences and ideas about those experiences within a series of continuous associations. These are coded by means of signs and symbols that may be referred to as the structure of the language. Whatever the kind of aggregate complex chosen out of these coded recordings, a dominant set becomes the controlling notion or idea for what each one terms as the "I". More specifically, in terms of name and form with which the identity is closest, or at least presumably to be so if not perhaps actually. Now, if this personality was restricted to this operational complex, even if it is given various labels and names, perhaps this would be a simple matter. In other words, it would be quite orderly for this "I" to function at the thought level and for feelings, emotions and experiences to function appropriately at any given point of time.

Unfortunately, the matter has not remained so orderly and with such clarity within the human system. For instance, any experience which happens for the first time is often a direct perception by the sensory organs. The next step is the registration of this experience and the sensation which is immediately coded and recorded within the total complexity, say, as being pleasurable or painful, comfortable or uncomfortable and so on. In other words, there is a mechanism whereby experience of pure perception or sensation is instantly translated into an idea or an image or any previous linguistic or other form of structure. It is then recorded in the brain cells; once again perhaps because of previous potentially recorded memories, as the propensities in the parents are already existing in the organism that goes back into times immemorial. Once an event is thus recorded it is transformed into "thought forms" — images, ideas, etc. — at the superficial level of consciousness. This recording is not only a kind of attribute but includes judgements of various kinds, of its relative worth due to comparison with some previous experience, or with some recorded ideal notions about what may be considered to be comfortable or uncomfortable, i.e. previous notions or experiences coded in terms of the nature of pain or pleasure. All this may have nothing to do with the actual experience or its perception. The nature of thought being the nature of memory, for the reason that in all that recorded and coded behaviour reference points or datum lines exist, that evaluate and judge. These evaluative processes, we are seldom conscious. All these methods of operation of the brain apply not only to feelings and emotions, they immediately operate as thought even in the perception of this physical seeing of object that appears to be "long" or "short" or "above" or "below" or "small" or "big" and so on. "Seeing" is also in the context of some measuring device consciously made in technical terms by society, working quite unconsciously, as a way of judging spatial and temporal evaluations about the external world.

We are doing all of this so constantly, quite unawares, and all the time within this framework of pre-existent categories learned in this socio-psychological conditioning. Perhaps, this is a good thing in the operational sense for it allows us to function instantly, as if naturally in everyday life. Thus, any signal of danger of say of a falling rock, the brain instantly judges the time and distance for the body to move aside with very accurate judgement. In this every day existence of survival — whether we call it instinctive or unconscious or ingrained thought patterns — no amount of thinking and measuring devices consciously help since that is a very slow process which would certainly put the lives of every person into jeopardy. The survival mechanism of both instinct and the learning of basic processes immediately get recorded to become the unconscious patterns if we want to function smoothly in routine everyday life without bringing into focus the so-called conscious thought which is the "I" or the Self-conscious person. This kind of illustration is true for various walks of life whether it is learning to ride a bicycle or driving a car or playing an instrument or writing or any other artistic work, or whatever skills are learnt, the smooth operation takes place later on, as if it were instinctive, a very natural process that emerging somehow by itself. Thus, at this operational level the task of measurement and judgement for the organism and any ideas about the organism are controlled in the deeper layers of the brain's system if it is to function smoothly and what we may call instinctively or spontaneously. However, the survival mechanism has become a psychological entity.

The body itself is the biggest measuring device for judgement of everything in life and in fact is a vehicle of consciousness. But its viewpoint in the mind is the viewpoint of the "I" with body as the focus. Whether psychologically one speaks of "my life" it is with reference to the body and the notion about its survival. The larger groups also use this organism as the reference point for the welfare of the society which is connected with the welfare of presumably the bodily existence of a large number of its members. It may be pointed out that if this was so, i.e. the body was considered to be the primary focus of welfare then greater care would be taken of it individually and collectively. We all know how despite contrary statements, the body is being used for its destruction not only in the way of various unnecessary addictions including overeating and so on, but in terms of tens and millions of people that are being killed and maimed by mankind today.

At any rate, the body's view is also the measuring device for the span of society or of the individual life or of the group in terms of number of years or generations, taking the average lifespan of the body. The number of years of measurement within the solar system, focused on the rotation of the earth, is also a judgement of the existence of this conceptualized lifetime of the bodily organism. It is obviously conceptual, only from the point of view of man, since it would be different if the lifespan of another animal species were taken into account. But within the universal scheme of things it is not an actual situation the way the macrocosm functions for at that level the lifespan of human measurement is quite insignificant.

At the physical level of existence such conceptual statements are essential for the organism to function in the environment it lives in. It has allowed man to have an enormous control over nature with the model of "domination–subordination". But control and exploitation of nature has shifted to that of human beings which has had disastrous consequences. This faculty of survival mechanism was once useful in the early stages of man's existence, i.e. the consciousness of learning the skills and techniques with an awareness of the past and an anticipation of the future needs and necessities as recorded and recalled from the memory pool. But this fragmentary area of the brain has continued to become an overspecialized part, separating itself into a psychological — thought — entity having outlived its utility a long time ago. It has moved on into the ideational plane, and these images and conceptual notions seem to no longer care for the human organism itself. But not only this, it was overtaken and blocked out the sensitivity of direct perception.

Sensations which are directly perceived are beautiful in experience for which the organism is well prepared. However, ideas and notions seem to intervene and interpret or conceptualize any experience that is taking place. Ideas and notions often block out the essential experiential nature of man within the harmonious flow of man–nature continuum. Feelings and emotions which man experiences whether these are of anger, frustration or pleasant ones are quickly labelled in the social set-up. This is not only by means of the word, but there is the essential ingredient of the socio-psychological judgement, conclusions of good or bad, right or wrong, what ought to be, should be or could be and would be, etc. This becomes the unconscious belief systems and traditions in which the so-called individual is socialized. For example, one is seldom "with" sensations or feelings, i.e. these are not allowed to be experienced since, no sooner these arise, through quickly searching from its memory pool, one passes judgement of its goodness or badness or whether this should take place or not. This process is repeated again and again unconsciously. There is constant measurement of values which arise from an amorphous social judgement that are ingrained into the personality, labelled as the "conscience of the individual". Thus, even the basic emotions which by themselves in a pure form are part of the existence of the human being are not alllowed to be experienced totally and completely. Ideas or thoughts are entangled with emotions and sensations. In fact one may go to the extent of saying that words, and images govern feelings and emotions since now coded emotions labelled as anger or happiness and so on, coded by words symbols are also judgemental whereby feelings and emotions are not experienced. For example, once some sensation or energy movement such as anger takes place within the organism and it causes discomfort of some kind; at that first instant one has learned from one's parents or from others, that it is called anger. The word is now recorded in the brain for this kind of sensation, although a similar sensation may not necessarily be "anger", except that it is given this label. Therefore, instant labelling of the word itself now triggers off both a judgement and a recall of those sensations, or

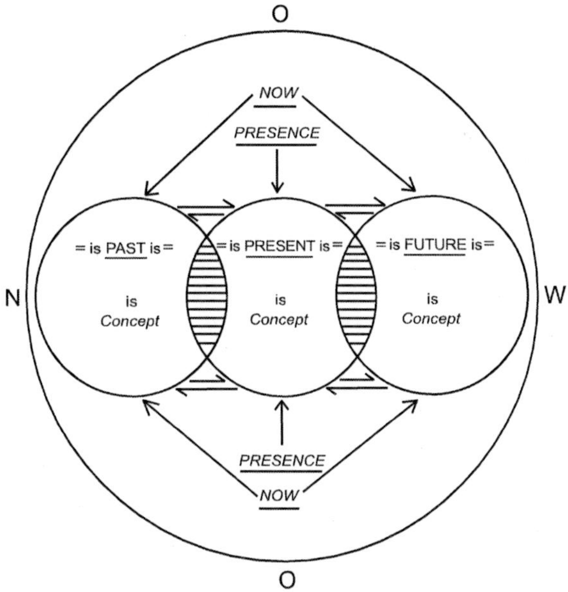

fig.7.2: Separation of thought from feelings and emotions can be erroneous

Explanation to *fig*. 7.2

Thus signs and symbols recorded in the complexity of language, memories which are the repository of the tens of thousands of traditions in a given society encoded in thought, which is a sophisticated form of material technology. We who are general in this overspecialization have become a series of ideas and images. In this way the physio-psychological structure in the notion of "I" is totally distorted. The body-brain or mental structure, this operational structure feels alienated, not clear and has become neurotic. It is then finally turning around in circles, or in this rat-race, looking or seeking in fact of who one is, not one thinks one is. It is difficult to break away from these shackles which have been there for so long that one believes these are part and parcel of me, of existence. One is so addicted to this known that the idea of freedom appears alien. The conceptual world is like frogs living in well and have no idea of a world outside it. That outside, that empty space that NOW, that PRESENCE is within which occurs all. It is the essence of life and that who one is, who we are. It envelops us moment to moment. It is like air, gravity and so on which allows for the context, concepts to happen. It is the ENERGY. ... $E\ mc^2$!

if sensations are experienced again in similar associations, then there is either no awareness; or there is no time to experience these sensations, since in the social set-up, thought comments: "you should not get angry, it is bad", etc. May be this separation of thought from feelings and emotions is itself erroneous (*fig*. 7.2).

Thus, signs and symbols recorded in the complexity of the language structure in fact become the repository of the thousands of years of tradition in a given society. This thought itself is a very sophisticated form of material technology, especially the more complicated and technological it becomes, such as in our own civilization, since the person even taking the body as a reference point therefore becomes only a series of ideas and images. Thus, the person herself/himself becomes a set of notions or an idea only. It takes him away from "consciously" experiencing even his feelings and emotions. This gives us an insight into the chaos or the disorder that has become a part of the psychological structure of most of mankind today. The body–brain system seems to be controlled fundamentally therefore by an idea, a very complicated idea at that, and which forms what is called a person or the "I". The operational entity itself is in fact not clear about its own existence and it does not act appropriately even in roles that it has to play on different occasions for a harmonious functioning within the natural and human environment. For example, even at the social level the person's role at work, at home or in any other social place is totally confused, for, most often the role which is appropriate at one point continues to be played at another time since the identification is so strong with a dominant role and its ideas. This is not given up in another situation. If a man holds a very high status in his office, it is often that out of official environment he perhaps continues to carry his status into the streets and also into the home, whereby now his role should be that of a husband and a father. It is commonly noticed that this appropriate role is not enacted, which results in futility, tensions and frustrations, both for the individual and society. Or, one carries frustrations prevalent in one situation say of the office, to give vent to them in the home atmosphere where it is totally out of place. There are numerous examples of this nature that are continuously happening in contemporary society. This outward disorder is a reflection of the inward disorder and chaos which is prevalent within the cortex itself. There is an overspecialized thought-technology — at one level — and that includes the technology of language, the complexity of ideas and images which become the sole object of the survival in the stream of consciousness, or at the psychological level.

The person, it should now be clear, is just an idea divorced from actual experience, feelings and emotions, far removed from the simpler sensations and perceptions. Not only this, the person is not even a "fixed idea", in the sense that the idea itself seeks continuously to wander for an elusive state of contentment or happiness to other ideas and notions since in the deepest layers the brain is aware of the dysfunctioning of itself and is constantly seeking, albeit erroneously, harmony and peace in terms of further improvement in technological structures which are mere chimeras. In this achievement-oriented system of the personality, of constant struggling, it causes further tension and frustration. The focus point now becomes one, knowing that this person, called the "I", is insecure and ephemeral, to outwardly continuously achieve or attempt to achieve some further elusive and utopian goal as if it is reachable and then "one day" there will be well-being. This constantly receding creation of goals sophisticates ideas about the supernatural, about God and heaven, etc.; these are the further creations of a disordered entity, whether it is a singular "I" or one which joins together to create further elusive and non-existent or functional entities such as nations or international bodies. The mind in this kind of ideational struggles for well-intentioned goals and objectives, or even freedom, is constantly in upheaval and disorder howsoever for peace and harmony it struggles so that the organism functions smoothly once again. In fact, words and the constant internal chatter become a kind of addiction for the supersensory organ, the brain, or more accurately a small part of the brain which has now become overspecialized. This is the dual movement of thought, by which is created fragmentation, i.e. there is a separation of "self" and "others".

8

The Dual Nature of Mechanical Thought

The Fragment and the Whole

CONSIDERABLE literature exists regarding the nature of the mind, about mental states, or psychological structure of the ego, the functioning of personality, as well as the nature of thought. It is not our intention to go into the genesis of such investigations. Our purpose is rather to look at thought from the vantage point of immediate experience, via an awareness of one's own self. Perhaps, in this way, the nature of thought shall be directly verifiable. In the context of the personal and civilizational crises, our emphasis is that each individual has to, by an acute possession of self-awareness, discover the functioning of the unit referred to as the "I". This involves the exercise of being an observer without judgements, beliefs, notions, ideas, images, etc. so that some direct perception comes about. Such could be termed as witnessing or choiceless awareness — what normally we would term as "non-action". In a nutshell, since the individual is veritably a unit of reality itself, it contains the universe within itself. If it makes a positive sign that says: "I am the world" or vice versa, only then has it the capacity to bring about a fundamental transformation. A mere change in this state of perception is by itself direct action. Thereby, the action is not only completely effective but perfect. This is not the normal definition of action, through ideas and dualities within which one functions. The normal — socially conditioned behaviour — appears to be hard work. But a glance at the last

5,000 years of human history shows that it has not produced the necessary results and as such in this sense is tantamount to inaction.

The "part containing the whole", idea may be illustrated by recent developments in holography and the formation of holograms. This is the production of a life-like image, not flat photographs, produced by light waves of extraordinary luminosity. These holograms are based on the principle of the relationship of "the part–the whole". In the hologram when visualized from different directions the view is as we normally see others. However, each segment of this hologram contains the same complete or whole image in the segment itself, even when it is separated from the totality, i.e. when one piece is sliced, in it the entire image is visible. It is said that when technological development will keep pace with this initial notion, that in a small one centimetre cubic square of such holograms the entire information today available to humankind not only from now but its entire past may be stored in this cube. The present storage systems of computers appear to be extraordinary since on a silicon tiny pinhead millions of information data are being already stored through laser beams. We can well imagine the information contained in each cellular structure, which may be like a replica of the universe itself.

At the physical level alone, though it is true at the psychosocial level as discussed earlier, the individual is a universal hologram; the so-called separate entity is the universe itself. Of course, the technology of language is all too inadequate, since it can only express the actual in terms of differentiation and separation. Once the mind seizes this perspective of "I am the world or the world is me" (or in old philosophical terms, there is only one without a second often stated in the word alone which means not isolation but what may be called "all-oneness"), then, the given perspective itself contributes to the transformation of the consciousness of the world. Consciousness is *what is*; within which all function. In the context there is no separate individual consciousnes of yours or mine, but a total stream of consciousness within which the body–psycho-social complex functions. Therefore, is it that this same awareness brings about a radical transformation in consciousness? It is like those waves which are created by throwing a pebble in a lake — they travel to the other shore without going anywhere. This is the natural way, being one with the bent of the universe, and not struggling against the stream.

Before adopting to this "natural way", an essential corollary is to develop a fundamental awareness about the movement against the stream in which mankind is caught up. A second nature today, we are hardly conscious of it. Hence, it causes a kind of entropy or genetic depression at all levels in terms of the evolutionary viewpoint. This holds true in the context of psychic well-being as well, that is, in terms of our relationship with the natural and biological environment, and so on. This movement is anti-life, anti-a-kind-of positive-energy, or life force. It is like one part of an organism or even a mechanism, going off at a tangent downhill due to its overspecialization. This is what causes not only aimless movement and destruction but also causes the major portion of the organism to falter and halt in its progress along the natural path. To use the metaphor of a bicycle, if one of its wheels gets dislodged to go off the road downhill, the rider starts to chase the wheel going downhill. He forgets the rest of the bicycle since chasing the wheel itself becomes an all-absorbing goal, without realizing the disastrous consequences of such an off-course movement of both contraption and rider. Even in everyday life a similar forgetfulness is common place.

To use still another parallel, we all know about the Chinese juggler who throws several plates into the air and keeps the momentum going with his hands. Often, one of the plates slips and falls down from his hands and breaks. A good attentive juggler takes up another plate rapidly and continues the movement. But most of us, as in the instance of the bicycle, are distracted when the plate falls and breaks. Instead of quickly replacing the plate with another to continue the movement, we try once again to put together the broken plate. In the process, the rest of the plates, which a good juggler will keep rotating, also fall and are broken to pieces. This implies that in the life process, several individuals —

mankind as a whole — seem to forget some essential movement of the life force that must go on rather than be digressed or distracted for what is lost. Psychologically, we do not like to give up the mistakes made, the resentments, regrets, allied memories, etc. We cling, grasp, or hang on to the lot. But then this takes us away from the dimension of living life fully, moment to moment — in the living present. This is what causes a dissipation of energy, a movement towards regression, stagnation or entropy, which forms a vicious circle of its own — a dog trying to catch its own tail!

The stress here is on this excessive specialization of a level of technology loosely labelled as mechanical thought. It includes — these logos — the ideas, images, signs, and symbols as are the groundwork or part and parcel of a total civilization — the external projections — complexity within which mankind is so caught up. Fragmentation and specialization have become an outgrowth of a small area of the brain. This causes a major part of it to deteriorate through sheer non-use. It is the functioning of this major portion which has in it universal qualities, a totality — a wholeness — which will allow mankind to be fully human once again. The overall functioning is however dominated by these outdated "survival mechanisms" that have really kept the species at a subhuman stage. It is a total erroneous labelling, of calling man a human being for the qualities of being human or even of what in essence is *beingness* is absent. It may perchance occasionally flower momentarily in some rare moments of one's life; yet, it is often easily dismissed as accidental or non-existent.

All that has been stated is perhaps very self-evident, if one pays attention to not only our own century but the last 5,000 years as well. We also know of a few far in-between rare individuals who had these qualities and, therefore, are remembered but not as human beings. They are remembered as saints, mystics or *avatāra*s, or those endowed with some other super qualities since the definition for most of mankind of normal human being really arises from a limited vision of their own selves, as a person, or "I". From the notion of separateness arise conflict and tension with all the other baser desires that are part of the quality of being normal or ordinary. This view is bound to be treated as true, since this topsy turvy perspective is part of our unconscious conditioning. This is the way one views one's own self and the world around us. It results in, shall we say the "frog in the well" habit, that creates an entire fictional or an illusion of what is called a real world. This separateness makes one completely forget one's essential nature, one's true relationship both within and to the external world. This exclusively mechanical way is what gives the feeling of being small and insignificant, of being incomplete. In this "unphilosophical" existence, there is the sense of being a mere fragment, a particle in the universe that makes little difference or is of no consequence. This is what creates the sense of alienation, separation and so on. A simple verification of the qualities of being human or a human being is the proportion of harmony — contentment and fulfilment — that is apparent or manifested not only within the individual but in relationship to other individuals and the environment.

This notion of isolation in itself is incorrect. Somehow, in the deepest recesses of one's psyche, there seems to be a knowing that this need not be so. But given the conditioning one attempts therefore to achieve fulfilment and completeness. Nevertheless, even when attempts are made there are wrong concepts and notions, such as, that each fragment by gathering many other fragments will become total and integrated; that greater information, knowledge, and effort will bring freedom. But this century has shown that with all the resources available, these efforts have been a failure, certainly in the psychological dimension. This specialization is an extension of the nineteenth-century notion of a solid factual world outside which if it were put together will form a complete picture. Thought — as ideation — is interlinked to this kind of momentum that is in a constant flow. With the building of such ideas one hopes to achieve completeness, wholeness and satisfaction. But all it does is to perpetuate itself. These enormous efforts only reinforce the old dimensions of previous psychological states that seek to grasp the mind in terms of the external world. Paths like this are blind alleys (*fig*. 8.1).

It is as if one day the achievements in the external world

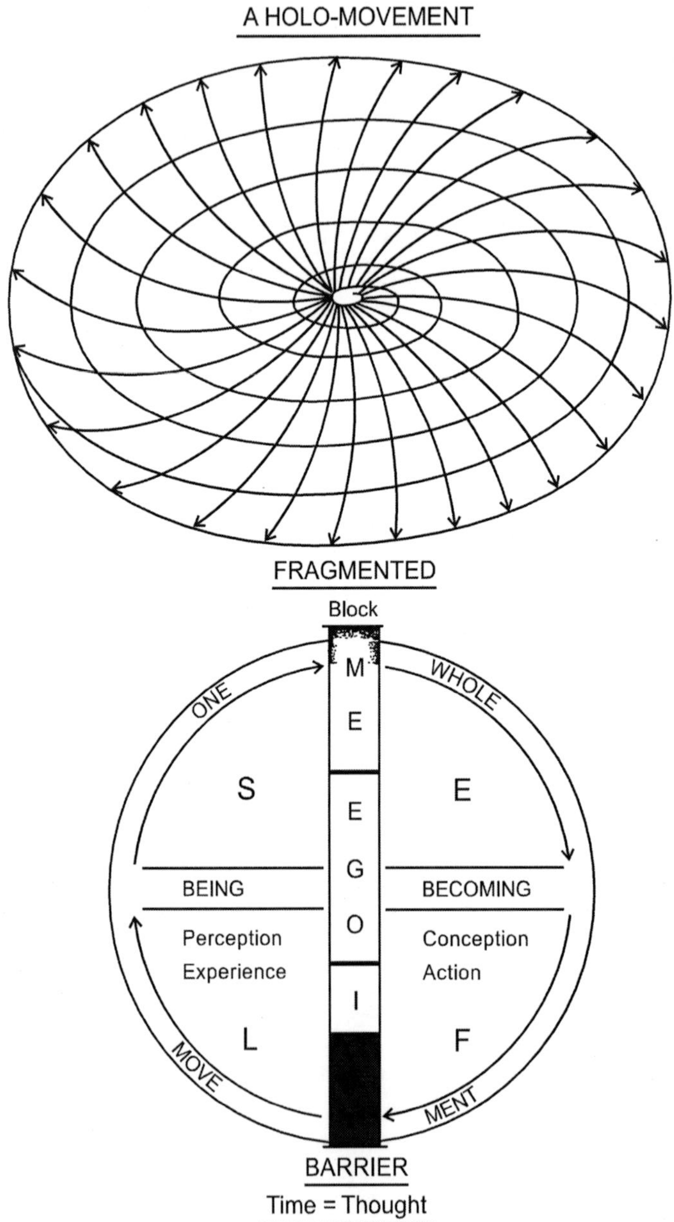

fig. 8.1: Being and becoming

Explanation to *fig.* 8.1

The world we know is fragmented although in reality it is a Holo Movement, a ONE whole or holistic movement. There are pure experiences unadulterated at first, and out of time. There is pure perception of the SELF, such as in listening to music or in the mountain, with nature or along the ocean. This is the expression Being, or Being-ness that is who we are, who one is. However, through or because of conditioning, all experiences turn into concepts because of language, thoughts, words–areas which are actually the foundation of the Ego. From childhood ideas and thoughts become or are the Me. This me or I turns all pure or first experiences into words because of socio-cultural conditioning in order to be comfortable with the known, the familiar, to make experiences of re-cognizable. In this way these concept then try to repeat the experience through the stored datas, memories. On this basis, action is then taken through logical steps, as if all pure experiences can be accessed again, in a constantly changing world. Nothing is repeatable. This seldom happens since these is a time lapse between the first act or experience, it is then stored as thought. and then action is taken, logically too many too many steps in linear times. This "me" "I" or thought or Ego becomes like a middle man intervening and become a barrier to that pure experience by constantly naming from the known memories or data base. This barrier or covering or veil or mask which is all a social product blocks all basic experiences and blocks any glimpse of the SELF that we are, or one is. This is the awareness, consciousness or witnessing consciousness that is who we are, who one is, blocked by linear time of the logical time that is constantly moving between what was and what should be.

shall, somehow naturally, bring about the elusive inner peace and contentment. First, one operates from a notion of fragmentation. Second, one wants to put together the separate pieces together, through the most intricate sophisticated national or international institutional organizations. But will the seeking by a part, separate from the whole (or other such divisions), produce the desired results? The linear mind cannot even see the context of the whole or a holistic mind which is diametrically different, not even opposite. The awareness of this very structure, of the false itself, is

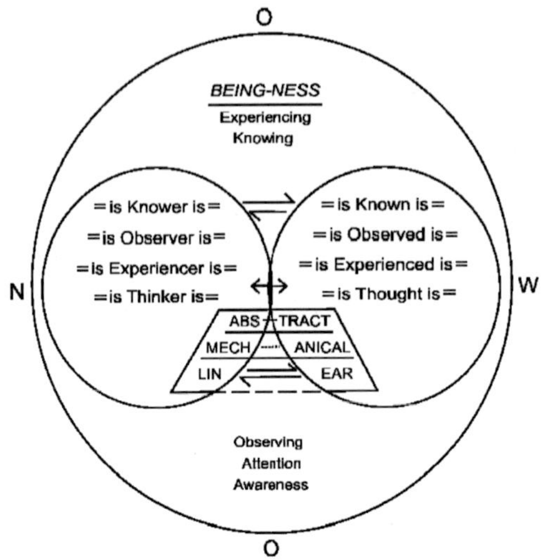

fig. 8.2: Beingness

Explanation to *fig.* 8.2

The little self or I as thought is a movement. In this context there is a movement from here to there, or of becoming something including realization. The me as thought has to become something. Its restlessness does not allow one to be present in the NOW. It creates that notion of grass is greener on the other side. It is all about the fact one is conditioned to believe that what is here and now is not ok so to move there from here to there mostly psychologically, and mentally becomes crucial in society. This is how one is brought up to believe, mostly because social upbringing is based on measurement, comparison and it is all relative. Thus all statements are comparative ones, all talks and conversation in the head refer to some benchmark or images of where one has to be. It is that little professor constantly judging oneself and others, between what could have been and what should be. That is becoming, plus living in dichotomies or dualities. This split is also the fact one is little aware of, that knower is the known, the observer is the observed, an experiencer is the experienced, the thinker is the thought. This is automatic, abstract mechanical linear mind that has been brainwashed. There are no such distinctions if one investigates or especially needs to be aware, observe choicelessly, give total attention to NOW. This moment, is what IS. In this way the Beingness, knowing, experience will be restored with no motive, no results, to just Be. To realize that all knowing is infact a non-verbal experience. It is only secondarily does this me takes over, pretending to be knower and doer. To be present, is the PRESENCE. It is to Re-member that is split because of fragmentation, this separateness. To be oneself again, to be whole, Holy once again.

a fundamental insight — it is the first stage towards the flow of the universe. Individuals with such awareness are complete, fulfilled and satisfied in a deeper sense of the word. Integrated within, it is a complete unit or one in its qualities of *beingness* that has the ability to produce an integrated world. The oneness by itself, on its own, spontaneously, transforms the universe by being present, i.e. the Presence transforms when there is no "I" (*fig*. 8.2).

Dichotomous Thought

Thought by its very nature, at the mechanical level of consciousness (or shall we say reactive unconsciousness), we are referring to is self-fragmentary. It only exists by creating dualities and by causing separation. This is its essential nature of what one commonly refers to as the person and "I". At that level it has even disengaged itself actually from the organism. All that it is, is an idea — a mental state — albeit unconsciously the body is still the reference point. Thus, the thinker, as the "I", becomes a non-stop commentary on the actual experience. This happens in an instant, the way one makes comparisons and judgements in terms of the social conditioning within which one functions. This is an incessant process; one of expectations, demands, ideas and images. It is the intricate world of illusion created and put into categories; the chief being that of language, words. Thought is constantly measuring. For this reason, the viewpoint, the line of measurement, is also continuously shifting, so that there is not even any actual constantness or continuity of the conceptual frameworks within which one functions.

At the level of survival in the external world thought is a necessity. But it shifts itself into psychological entities, where the "I" itself is a series of societal ideas and images, within what is called as one's self wherein the interaction — or mere chattering — takes place constantly. In order for the movement of thought to maintain itself, it is continuously searching for solutions, for measurements, regenerating more problems, more ideals, etc. But no complete solutions are possible, as it is never, to start with, complete by itself. The brain functioning only at the ideal level is rarely in tune — or "with it", with the actual experience totally or completely. If it does so, this implies putting away — in abeyance — all thought or the "I". Will thought allow this?

For this to happen it means the dropping away of all comparisons and measurements, i.e. the notion of "I". This is what allows for direct insight or perception to operate for the various life forces potentially evident in the brain to fully function, without searching into memory pools of what is already known and its continuation. Thought travels and wanders between what was and what ought be. It even passes judgements on what is already in terms of the known. In doing so it loses touch with the present on knowing fully what is in the now. There is this dual movement all the time, "from here to there", no different to physically going from here to there as a movement of time and space. The external world — physical — is a projection of this movement. In any case, even psychologically the movement is from here, the known, i.e. from what is here, to a movement of what is to be achieved, or there, fulfilled as an ideal. But the latter is also known as an image arising out of past experience. In all walks of our life, this is the operational game. Therefore, between *what is* direct perception and direct action, there is the creation of the concept of time and space. This movement itself does not allow for experience, instant perception or "seeing" as "action" to come into existence. This barrier, the separation, does not allow for life to fully operate as true action. Being anti-life the goals necessarily and constantly recede further and further. The movement is from known to the known — from a dead past to a dead future — not a freedom of going into the unknown or the impossible.

Thus the seeking — at an abstract, ideal, thought level — of satisfaction, fulfilment, completeness is an exercise in futility. But with thought — as "I" — this is an obsessive drive, this sense of goals, of achievement, whether it is physically, emotionally or through what is called spirituality. The intentions may be good, but such is the way to hell! The impossibility of "seeing" this situation is out of grasp without "awareness" or "attention". And any awareness is not possible when the mind is constantly wandering. When it is constantly occupied, it is like seeing the world from a shaking vehicle hoping to obtain clarity but without stopping a shaking body. This conception of wandering also exists in ideas and images, in the day-to-day physical world to become an addiction. This is the neurosis of escape, of day dreaming where the brain cells are repeatedly stimulated by words and images. It is so strong that what we are stating here becomes an impossibility even for the sake of mere consideration. Any reference of the individual is now at this addiction level. It is in the language or words that are used to make several pronouns for itself — this non-entity. For example, one may notice in the dialogue that goes on within the mind, "one" is "I" and the use is purposely to state it as a pronoun for a name, although normally it is the first personal noun, yet it is not beyond referring to the same personality. It is totally inaccurate since there are no two persons. But not only is the dialogue which in a normal person goes on in the head in terms of the "I" or one's name, there is yet another sentence that follows that often says "you should not do this" or the "I" becomes "we" or "us" and "you" becoming "they", "them", etc. There is thus this constant false duality of several persons. It itself is the creator of misery and suffering, far removed from actual misery or suffering if there be any. The cause of a major chaos or disorder in the brain is this projection of fictional entity or entities that also appear very strongly to be manifested in terms of the coded imagery of this ideal of bodily comfort and discomfort. But since the master controller is itself malfunctioning, can either peace or true action take place? Actually, if one pays even a little attention, are there really several voices or thoughts — uncontrolled — appearing by themselves out of nowhere and disappearing into nowhere? Are these not merely words, and without even sounds of what we call voices?

The Dual Movement

By sheer observation, attention, awareness, we have noted that signs and symbols have become a major vehicle of not only communication with the outside world but what goes on within an individual head. There is a movement of these words whereby a constant dialogue takes place. In fact, there is a close identity of the person with these movements of thoughts. Thought creates the thinker! There is no separation between the person and the thoughts as most of us seem to believe. For example, we are in the habit of referring, not only to one's body as "my body" but also "my thought" and so on. It is as if there is one self or the "I" which is the subject and it has an ownership that is referred by the pronoun "my". This is with regard to the body and thoughts — in many ways body and thought being synonymous, i.e. body being a thought form. In any case, this is not a different manner to one's ownership of such other external objects as the clothes one wears, or such other, status positions like "my wife, my husband, my house, my children", etc. at the level we are talking. But is there such a separation between the "I" and "me" or "mine"? Is this not linguistic jugglery? In the context of movement of thought the reference to the "I" or "mine" is a notion, concept, idea and images which are put together in the total context of the social, mental and other cultural conditioning. This is what creates an aggregate of ideas with perhaps a dominating one which controls the various selves, including all the roles it plays. These ideas or more appropriately societal attributes which are conceptualized in language are the thoughts that are being recorded within the brain. Do then these as a physico-psychosocial entity not enact out the role of a sophisticated input–output computer system?

The various labels — the attributes — in the given social system have all the time a reference point which is coded in one word, "I" or "self". In other words, form, name and images are all within the social system, i.e. the label is absolutely the result of social and cultural norms. the aggregate of the said notions is in the "I" itself. Is there without attributes or concepts, any "I"? Now this aggregate of thoughts or thought forms called "I" with such and such attribute or name (as opposed to all the other notions and concepts which are different at variance, and/or are compared with some ideal) becomes another person or a group that is referred to as "others", i.e. "the self and the other". The separation is then made of "I" with all its attributes and identities, the various inner and outer, all expressed in terms of symbols of society and culture. The context arises out of the wider concepts of family, tribe, nation or professional activities, or whatever else. And, the others are "they" with whom comparison is made in a relative state of measurement that is an ideal norm, or an abstraction of the state of things.

There then seems to be played this game — within the brain cells as sensation — with this structure of signs and symbols, other categories, which differ from one social group to another. This reflects one viewpoint or another, a reference to "oneself" or the "other". These various entities are focused around some ideal norms and values often referred to as the "social conscience", voices or thoughts that appear in one's head as if out of nowhere. These from time to time are modified by one individual and then may be incorporated by several others to become different sets of values. This new social consciousness or conscience once again socializes new individuals as a continuous process.

At any rate, within the individual's head there are at least these two things going on, generally two categories, whereby a continuous dialogue takes place. It is between what is now taken to be granted as the "I" — a pronoun for the name — and one voice which refers to the same "I" by the pronoun "you" in the context of what you should have or ought to have done or not, etc. There may be many more such voices, or thoughts that keep up the superficial movement of the "I" thought continuously. Each person seems to be entangled in these various surface movements of thought as stated by the network of ideas and images, linguistically structured. A majority of the dialogue is between what "should" and "ought to be" that is so ingrained in the socializing process. There is a continuous flow of information and reaction which one may refer to as the input and output system. This is how decisions(?) are taken or a choice(?) is constantly placed before one. The confusion of decision-making arises within this duality of what the individual wants or desires and what he should be doing according to the norms in which he is brought up. Actually what one wants or desires is often also the surfacing of some deep social conditioning. After all, is there yet another entity that is to "choose", "decide" and so on?

If one notices, there is only one thought at a time, or a string of words put together. Yet these are so rapid that it seems as if there were several thoughts or voices taking place simultaneously. Apparently there is an incalculable fast pace for thought to form and to state itself at all levels. At one time thought had a great adaptive and functional significance in the early stages of mankind and its control over the enemies in the natural environment. The speed of experience translated into thought, the comparison of it with the recorded memory, of anticipation and action seem to take place almost as if instantly.

The movement of this kind of dual mechanical thought — now the self-conscious "I" — takes place at the psychic level as a dialogue between at least two linguistic categories with either of which one identifies as one's self, as continuous statements or commentary on whatever one is experiencing even at the feeling and emotional level. At every instant there is labelling, a commentary in the context of unconscious not only ideals but other experiences of pain and pleasure, fear and anxiety and so on. It is all like an automaton. The notion of the "I" as an idea with all its ramifications, howsoever widespread these identities may be, has taken over by and large the role of the survival mechanism of the species into one that operates for its own survival. Often, the dialogue is between the hindsight and the perpetuation of those notions into a future, a projection of anticipation of such identities and their associated expectations and demands. In this process, the present experiential level is totally lost. It is a game of fear of pain, or imagined pain, of a previous experience and its concept. It is then an attachment to the concept, the loss of such concepts now becoming an attribute of that label or name, given to that particular form that wishes itself perpetual continuity even after the physical form has disappeared. The actual experiential or appropriate functioning is somehow totally forgotten even at the expense of the existence of the body, for whose healthy functioning thought developed. The body is put in jeopardy since its existence becomes of little consequence in the game of the perpetuation of the idea or thought itself. Physical pain may or may not last for long. Its mental recording continues and this memory continuation is what is actually suffering, i.e. the fear and anxiety of the pain as remembered or as projected. This mental state as thought — is the "I" entity that uses the body, pretending an identity with it.

To take quite simple examples from everyday life, even when one is eating or drinking or one has a desire for a certain kind of drink, it arises from a previous experience that has been recorded as a notion, as a memory in some formula or model. It is recalled as a part of the desire to repeat that experience once again. Whatever the association or "recall mechanism" — even a so-called physiological need — the desire for a certain food or drink or any other material or emotional bond arises from this recorded memory of a previous experience that occurred though often perhaps without any previous conscious knowledge of it. Of course, one may say that these potentialities exist within the vast reservoir of the individual's existence. One may have probably fully experienced it totally with all of one's sense perceptions, without any concepts or thoughts arising. But once this takes place, instantly there is a translation into a language, of its nature of pleasure or pain, comfort or discomfort and so on. The latter ideas are also in some ways socially learnt and are built into the conditioned body–brain mechanism. From this recorded experience, the second time any desire and thought arises it is to repeat the same experience; whether soon after the first one or even after twenty years because of some other reactivation in the programming. During the second time the experience takes place by the comparative method which says that this time it is not as good as the first time or it is better or some such other recall of associated thought forms. This then is the repetition of thought about that experience which is taking place as a reaction, mechanically, and not experientially in the sense of a first-time experience. One might say that it is a recorded thought or a commentary which is mechanically repeating itself as a kind of addiction of the brain itself. It is almost like a thought or a concept of eating or drinking or experiencing some more thoughts and concepts which are stated in the careful guise of experience. This is to show how our daily living "experiences" at the superficial level are with the identity of a self which is an idea or an image. Various ideas formed in this manner take the organism away from its healthy functioning which is by itself one of the sheer joys of life experiencing itself and its surroundings.

It is within this separation of an "I", the idea or an image, that all other notions of "action" or "inaction" of perception and so on occur. It is with this perpetual movement of words, and behind it the meanings and deeper images — this entire range is the movement of thought — with which one identifies. This would be all right as far as it goes if one became attentive to the fact that there is no separate "I" from thought itself. Therefore to "see" amounts to the transformation of the perspective. An awareness of the veil of ignorance gives an insight with what has caused agony, misery and suffering. But it is not only that this separation has to be given up, but also the constant desire of thought not to be with the experience. Thought is absent in a totally holistic and fully experiencing state. This experience of the organism is itself a threat to thought, for the survival of the idea and the image. Mechanical thought by its very nature only functions by creating its opposites. Being totally with the experience, creates no opposites. This is why it is difficult to be "with it" as one notices. It perpetually wants to be elsewhere than where it is, since it is a function of comparisons only. It is this kind of a game that has become an addiction for the brain, perhaps, this is why it is painful for the organism and its survival. It may thus be clear that memory becomes the source of the identity of the self. But a great deal of all this arises from the fundamental fact that thought does not allow a total and complete functioning of any action, since if this were the case there will be no residue left to form an incomplete action, to become another desire for future thought, whereby thought could thrive. This

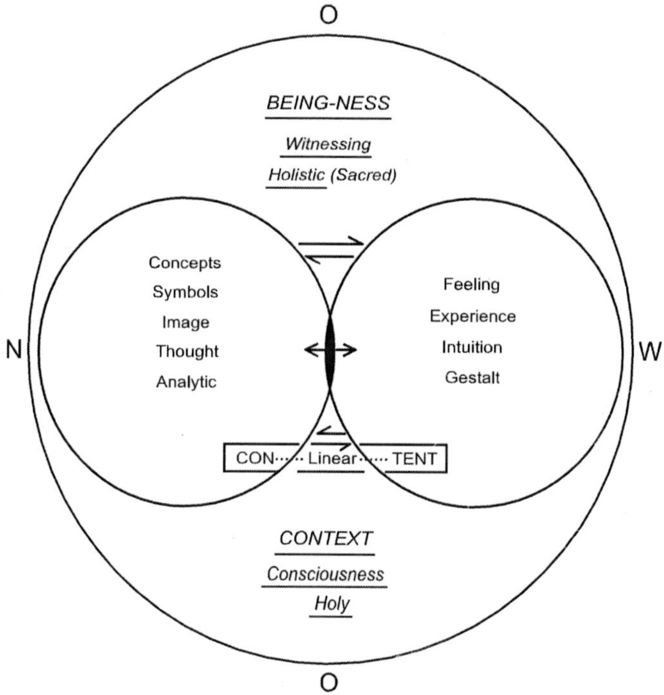

fig. 8.3: Witnessing

Explanation to *fig*. 8.3

Within the context of NOW within the head-mentally within Being-ness, Witnessing Consciousness, within the Sacred Holistic, Holy Consciousness, the Context of Contexts is present Content or operational thought which is of duality and functioning mechanically, within the relative world, the illusion or Maya. Thought as language, words is conceptual. It has symbols, images, logical as rationality (expressed according to the cultural conditioning) within linear time, the left brain whereby most of the modern world is running. Because of this dominating Cartesian dictum "I think therefore I am", the world is out of balance, creating the havoc and disasters we see all around, it suggests the old saying "whom the gods wish to destroy first make them mad"

A balancing can happen through contemplation awareness, choicelessly. It is to be aware of the left brain which is intuitive, pure feeling, experiencing, Gestalt. The two spheres, often labelled as feminine and masculine or Yin-Yang, are going their own way, in fact the intuitive self is being ignored in the modern set up. The dictum therefore is "I am therefore there is thinking and the rest". It is to be noted that the non-verbal non-intellectual reflected are in the areas as music, painting, dancing, poetry, making pottery, cooking, working with hands in the field, and so on. The emphasis on technology and economic is destroying the creativity aspects of the brain or mental set up. Thought itself is a very sophisticated technology, is matter needs one to be aware of, is matter located in the brain cells. Unfortunately this specialization has taken over, it is the ego, along with emotions and everything that are encoded. It has overshadowed this creative intuitive self or Self. It avoids being in the present, to continue the movement, coming from a state of incompleteness, to tasks unfinished at the very end. Because being present totally does not leave any residue. It leaves one to function fresh and alive moment to moment. The restlessness of all kinds becomes the baggage which one carries to know that this is the "me" of interpretative memories, the image, the unreality, the falseness, of being a mirage, a dream-world. The awareness of all this stated above allows for Freedom, Freedom from the known as J. Krishnamurti states so clearly.

is the addiction of all addictions which is not easily given up, since "growing up" is also part of the same game. The external addictions are a by-product of the mind game! The mind is always after what it has not got, away from what it has *now*, whatever it might declare to the contrary.

Thought — or "I" — therefore does not allow anyone to be completely with one moment of *here* and *now*. Or, it allows an action which is almost complete and for some justifiable explanations does not allow it to be completed so that it may be repeated mechanically, and thought itself can then perpetuate itself. To leave things incomplete, and to create opposition is the characteristic of thought. Both incompleteness and duality allows a mechanical repetition as well as a perpetuation of the recorded pleasure and pain principle whereby desire, fear and anxiety may continue on and on in this stream of consciousness. Thought itself is thus a concept of space and time within which the "I" or the person is not a separate dimension. Functioning without thought is to be in yet another totally different dimension. The eternal silence is fundamental to the quality of wholeness of one's being and that most of mankind has missed in this entanglement, in this movement of thought. Deep thought becomes identical with beingness when no opposites are created in tune with and subservient to wholeness (*fig*. 8.3).

We have thus learnt that thought is a continuous movement of various ideas and images placed within the structure of language. At this level the origin is within the social system that conditions all of these notions and concepts. These, when put together, form a nucleus of what is called a "person" with various conceptual attributes related to sensory perceptions that interact with the external world. The observer therefore is a reaction to the external stimuli which are then categorized and formulated into certain notions. The sense perceptions include the sense organ of the brain in a larger meaning; they are all a product of all the elements of which the external world is itself made up. Without the external stimuli there would be no internal response, neither the sensory nor the neurological one. To put it this way would also hold true for a statement like "the observer is the observed". This is true too with regard to the thought which arises from all the recordings of, to put it simply, stimulus–response mechanism. These are sorted out from moment to moment within the memory pool which as far as we know is recorded in the brain cells. In this recording not only are there the experiential events or the first experiences but the experiences of both pleasure and pain known from the earliest times, even before physical birth. However, there are also the secondary recordings of many layers over this primal or primary level of recording that lead to even tertiary ideas and images.

The primary experiences may be taken to be total experiences of completeness — or of full satisfaction — which are present in most children from the earliest age. This, since the mind is an open-ended system inclusive of the body. This experience may be a feeling of comfort or discomfort, which in itself is an experience. Yet in the social set-up, parental admonitions–rebukes or other similar pointers towards conduct are signals of different or contrary concepts regarding these primary experiences. The brain from now on with any of its experiences, immediately connects it with some other social–parental association. This experiencing becomes a kind of a linear connection of cause-and-effect rather than a complete moment of the *now*. This part of the mind thus arranges all experiences in a linear sequence, or what is called linear kind of cause, a linear effect, confined within the philosophy of a "survival" mechanism; to place all experiences within this framework. For example, if an early experience of a certain pleasure at a given point is connected to a sensation (like some colouring) or the smooth sense of the clothing which his or her mother is wearing at that point of time, then that sensation is immediately connected in the brain to the experience of pleasure at a given segment of time, and recorded as such for future references. Many years later, the same adult re-experiences pleasure somehow seeing a similar coloured pattern, or experiencing the sensation for smooth clothing material somewhere or on some other person, without conscious knowledge of the association. He or she will instantly like it. This is so with each event; it is the experience for the person with which the primary experience has been recalled or brought to the surface many years later. It will be referred in such terms as "some inexplicable reason of liking that event or person". Similar sensations of displeasure or discomfort and "not liking another person" or situations are also recorded within this framework of the primary recording of early childhood of the primal experience within the total set-up. Much prior to this, the potentialities for receiving and discarding signals are in-built into the genetic material.

Within this survival mechanism of pleasure/pain, approval/attention, or pain/avoidance of pain and fear and anxiety — all these early conditional notions build up all the other secondary and tertiary experiences which are recorded as ideas and images in what is called "thought". It is to be noted that there is no actual connection between thought and action that it builds up even though appearing to be so because of the linear mind's nature to do so for its own continuity and perpetuation. The linear mind does so for its survival or whatever it identifies with as the notion of survival. Thus, the mind takes the body as a reference point which we believe is often the case. It will do anything in terms of these associations to make its survival through the body or whatever its notion on the pleasure-seeking notions of the sense organs of the body which the mind is really enjoying. But if the mind, along with its body, identifies with concepts of family or of nation, a flag, a symbol or even several slogans, and indeed even its own name which as an idea it wants to survive because it identifies with it, then the body is of little consequence. This then is what may be called martyr complex, or working for posterity. It is for this reason of the projection of survival identity with concepts and images that have sent millions of people to bodily deaths and killed others for the sake of a name or a flag or some other slogan or ideology. It is common to see men doing work on a basis which suggests that during their lifetime or the lifetime of their bodies this work will not be completed, and then sacrifice the present state of their functioning for an idea, for the sake of posterity which can include family, children or larger entities like nations or other imagined states where their names will be remembered in some research or other organization; or he or she may be sacrificing his or her life to uphold some ideal and tradition and so on. The idea for this linear mind, it to survive even at the expense of sacrificing the body or the present state of "aliveness", completeness and full satisfaction. The conditioning of the linear mind is so strong to this seductive chain of cause–effect that it cannot see itself any other way, i.e. taking into account that the structure of the mind, including the body, functions holistically in total "moments of now". In short, the ideal of holism cannot be understood by the linear mind.

Most of humankind at present is caught up within a small sphere of the brain which thinks in the linear manner of which mechanical thought is the chief tool and vehicle. This is why most individuals by not living in the "now", live in appalling frustration or dissatisfaction. In this false manner of chasing images, or one's own shadow in which an actual substance is being attempted to be found, mankind looses a great deal of its peace and harmony, or that state of tranquillity which is crucial if one is to get out of both the personal or the civilizational crises. It is this linear model within which thought functions that is the chief cause of trouble. Those other secondary complex situations are today externalized because of the same chaotic and confused thought processes.

For example, thought processes associate happiness with the external concepts and notions materialized in terms of goods of various kinds, food and drink and all the other utilitarian and consumerism, so prevalent in the world today. But we have enough experience to note that this is a false association — of a certain psychological "state of being" — with these external material conditions which themselves arise from certain notions of what we deem to consider "action" erroneously as bodily comfort and discomfort. But that is the way the linear mind works, totally falsifying the picture and demanding to chase mirages, shadows and images which it covers for its own sake in several veils as if this were the essence for some tangible "solid" stuff. All such mind stuff is really imaginary, with little substance to it. Each one of us needs to be aware that from early childhood how thought makes us connect these false associations not only to produce the so-called "self" or "person" as if it were real, but also endlessly pretending as if tomorrow or on a certain day that state of happiness and feelings of being well, shall finally arrive if only one were to follow these and other rules, acquire those and all the other conditioned responses for which society lives; in other words, all the same kinky images.

The truth of this is seen in the common statement that "one day after finishing school there will be fulfilment, and happiness and life will go smoothly". But as one reaches that so-called goal, the vision recedes further in a kind of regression of a false concept of the practical life which once again states "once I finish college, once I get a job, once I get married, once I have children, once these children grow up, once these children get married and once I have grandchildren and finally one day when I retire I will have a house and live happily ever after". This is the recurring theme of an evasive or illusive philosophy, the one of a linear mind; this is the mind's way of survival at the expense of life, aliveness even, and self or the body–brain mechanism.

It is the experience of everyone from the lowest to the highest that it is good to reach great heights, or also acquire name, fame, wealth and position in the world. But this state that of "one day" when there will be happiness and satisfaction may be elusive and non-existent. This is why, stemming from this same psychological state each one at whatever position, without any of this quality of aliveness and feelings, somehow feels he/she is not making any difference to the quality of life. He or she who desires the outward appearance, yet knows it fully within his or her heart of the emptiness and hollowness of such illusory perspectives through the externalized material things which are really only concepts or thought projections fundamentally without any grounds, of any association with "states of being". Consequently, millions today chasing such false notions of the linear mind produce misery and suffering. Pooled together this vast effort becomes the stream of consciousness of humankind in general on a global scale, in which we are all caught.

This state of affairs exists in every direction socially, and even emotionally in one's relationships. Each one imagines that some other person or persons contribute to some other's well-being since even this cause–effect mechanism works at a relational level. Given the notion, one believes that at moments of similar state of thought, mind or heart — and which coincides between two people — there is a relationship, and "I" or "the other" is the cause of this beautiful feeling and the formation of a relationship which will not only now, but always bring happiness. Since this is once again a false proposition there is soon disillusionment at this level as well. And seeing that, the very person becomes the cause of unhappiness and misery. This is one and the same principle of being a victim, of seeking pleasure and fighting pain by attributing causes to other persons and things. In the reverse level, one attributes being a victim at the hands of other people and being victimized by the circumstances and social situations.

The answer in the normal work of a linear mind to this is

once again to change the circumstances or the environment or the people around on to whom is attributed the cause of our misfortunes and unhappiness, not dissimilarly to the notion that the other people are the cause of one's happiness. The idea is, then, restated in terms of the "one-day philosophy" when changes are made; or then "there will be that same quality of happiness or well-being, once I change house, job, location, partner or take a holiday".

It is so for several thousands of years that man has been attempting to achieve fulfilment within the framework of this linear mind, especially so in this century when so much resources are available. The irony, or the cleverness of mechanical thought at this level, is that the veils do not allow one to wake up to the dreadful fact of living in illusions. In fact, most of humankind is in a state of dream living at the subhuman level of a "action–reaction" system or a stimulus–response system arising from deep conditioning that is a long heritage of a total racial, mental and memory pool within the stream of consciousness that continuously reinforces itself. This negative stream of consciousness contains all the fears, and all the anxieties, the desires and wants created by thought itself. It does so at the cost of a full human being, who may really only be fulfilled and satisfied in "moments of now", for in doing so lies the ability to clear up all the sundry life problems (naturally in the process of life or living itself). Perspective and direction have simply got to be changed along the direction of "the way", or the flow of the river, which itself is a transformation of 180°, and allowing naturally without any effort or struggle, to transform everything including oneself into a state of harmony. But man erroneously believes that he has to struggle and make an effort against the flow, as if going up the old stubborn stream will get one anywhere. The goal is in the other direction — that flow of the river going downstream which will take one onward naturally, into the great ocean, or the eternal source wherein lies the immensity of eternal values which each one — as who am I? — is in fact truly searching separately and collectively. This perception itself is action.

9

Who Am I?

THE question — who am I? — has of course been raised from times immemorial. Here, the attempt is to discuss it not only in the context of the evolution of man–society continuum, between the microscopic and the macroscopic elements as an abstract logical argument as stated in the previous chapters, but also in that of one's everyday experience, in the wake of full attention. In relating it this way it is easier to probe deeper into these ideas by one's own activity at all levels rather than through second-hand sources. Knowledge then becomes verifiable through one's own experience. It may then be corroborated by similar experiences in the lives of other people as intellectual statements or in other forms of symbols, signs and cultural expressions that differ from society to society (Eliade 1962).

The word "I" signifies a mental statement of certain attributes and characteristics designated by a name given socially and with reference to a form, which is the body. This is the psycho-somatic structure. At the physical level mental concepts are put together in the form of a series of thoughts, which have unconscious or subtle reference to the mechanics of the organism — including both the body and brain structure. The name refers to the body for, when one says "I go" or "I come" or any such statement even of "my attachment", the reference is to the body and its movements or its attachments at the mental level with reference to the family, say, children or wife or husband; all of it means the body and its functions in terms of sensory perceptions and sensations (Nisargdatta 1973). It is as if the body — the human form — is the "matter of fact", "I" the mental statement. This is taken for granted as a reference point and it includes all other bodily forms to which it is interrelated on the planet. In fact, the body is a viewpoint of the physical earth from which it has emerged. It is therefore no surprise knowing that not only is the point of view man-centred but also earth-centred in any other larger context as well. It is almost as if the earth is viewing the universe through its products from different angles. But these are essentially, we may do well to remember, mental notions.

Further the notion of mental states is known because of consciousness. Therefore, consciousness has to be present in the elements of the earth itself in order for it to exist within man who emerges and is formed out of the same stuff. It is a manifestation of earthly consciousness expressed in the different creatures and perhaps the highest point being as far as we believe or imagine, present in mankind. But somehow because man walks and lives around the earth with his various technological developments (of which he seems to be so proud as his own creations), that he has forgotten his links to the foundation which sustains it. Because of these abilities he seems to feel that rocks, trees, birds or animals are closely bound to the earth and not he, because of his gift for rapid movement. But he is equally tied to the earth and its consciousness which has produced him. He is the earth, and he is the consciousness.

Unfortunately man has forgotten not only his ground of being which is consciousness, but in this thought-oriented technological advance, the body-centredness is taken for granted, that prevents individual enquiry into "who am I" (Osborne 1974). All the references of the "I" are in the context of body and its ramifications in terms of concepts and ideas that form the essence within this unconscious manner of existence to a mere survival notion — a trifle. But a little attention to this question easily reveals that until there is mental awareness of the body there could be no idea that we are body-centred. That is to say, some mental apparatus makes one aware not only of bodily existence which refers to the "I", but conceptual and symbolic representation with attributes is essential at the mental level. It is the putting together of all social conditioning into the notion of "I" or the self. A little deeper investigation already tells us that the body is a product of spatial and temporal interrelationships and developments of the physical universe that is operating and impinging upon him, as we know it today, whatever the theoretical dimensions for the explanation of this phenomenon may be, i.e. that is logically "given" in any "contemporary" situation. The mental action–reaction system at the thought level of what we call as self-consciousness is once again the consequence of spatial and temporal extensions of all kinds of conditioning which exists in the totality of the memory pool of racial or ethnic memories of humanity. In other words, at the physical and mental level the self is a product of everything throughout the entire spatio-temporal duration. Thoughts include emotions and feelings and other experiences that arise from unconscious depths of what is called the unconscious. Actually it is all consciousness and which in explanations of the current state of knowledge have divided into so many categories. But in the absence of deeper awareness for most of our lives, even the experiences are unconscious in nature as the process of living itself is at the survival level. Therefore, there is no time to contemplate, to look deeply within any kind of choiceless observation with regard to oneself or the world. Normally, what one calls living is through this mechanical and repetitive dimensions controlled by the narrow areas of thought which has given rise to the "I". In this false manner one believes that one is awake, "alive and conscious". The elusive personality or the "I" is also taken for granted to be an eternal entity which has become the foundation of the way civilization and its working — or not working!

As already stated, it is clear that there is no such separateness of this person or "I", whether mentally or physically. The separation is a conceptual one in order to facilitate everyday operational areas of daily living. But when an operational entity with many roles is taken to be fixed, endowed with real existence, then this false premise creates in almost geometric proportions further illusory or false dreams and nightmares. The dualistic notion is an attribute of thought and it contributes psychologically to this untrue notion. Not until a certain sense of awareness is developed that it becomes possible to see the truth of this situation. The self and seeker are tempted to search in the world by all kinds of actions and plans to reveal the truth of the "I". Given a little deeper inquiry one will find that the "seeker is the sought". This is like the peeling of an onion layer by layer to see the truth of it, which shows that after all the layers are removed there is in fact nothing there.

The discovery is startling and shocking at first for it is the beginning of a collapse of an entire world, which now appears as building castles in the air (Watts 1972). It is a great threat since the kind of false security that one imagined in which one lived or one hoped to live in has not or does not exist and will not come into existence. It is an awakening and a shock to thought itself and a stage which may be called transition of "no man's land", twilight zone; an area of darkness with a kind of awareness unlike the previous states of unconscious living and experiencing. In fact, from this awareness the earlier state appears as total darkness, though in the unconscious living, one believed one was "awake" and alive. This transitional state which means a cutting off of links, even if these were false is a state of disturbance and like the first moment of waking up from sleep, one does not want to face the incoming light or the prospect of having to consciously start the day for work. This unconscious sleep is what seems peaceful or a lazy way of passing away one's life, for basically the mind at this level always tries this kind of escape mechanism even if it is falsely claiming "action" or activity of life. This is why often people who have experienced a slight kind of awakening often do not believe those moments and fear those brief moments, as being afraid of one's own non-existence as a name and form; to seek the slumber of unconsciousness once again. Because, in these moments, yesterday and tomorrow are unknown, which is an actuality. But the initial experience is awesome and often terrifying, of this stark "nothingness".

Even at the practical level the knowledge of the "I" — which can easily be verified — is very little known to one, though one may claim to know much. For instance, without going into the previous paragraphs one may ask questions about one's body which one claims to be "mine" or the "thoughts" as "mine". None of us has ever seen one's own eyes or any other part of the body, as one sees another person whom one faces. Even the mirror shows a reflection and that too is true in terms of the state of mind which is revealed in terms of concepts that frame our perceptions. Obviously, as we have stated elsewhere, visual perception is governed by the imagery within other frameworks existent in the mind. So, how certain one is of even this elementary existence becomes doubtful. Although there is nothing, there is no knowledge — objectively speaking — and even much less so of the functioning of the body that we claim to be ourselves. For it functions without any knowledge on our part. Thus, without any conscious knowledge or even a minute idea about the functioning of sensory perceptions we claim certain — implicit — ownership of it (*fig*. 9.1).

The same is done in the case of thoughts which once again come and go like the body; both these come and go within their own laws and their nature. Even during dreams seldom or never does one see one's own body although one sees everything else, as during the state of being awake, as if it is outside oneself. The dream seems equally real while we are dreaming and then the notion of time is also a dream time. Although when one wakes up it is only then that we call it a dream. From the waking angle what seems an age is only perhaps an existence of a minute or two. Of course, in a deep state of sleep which most of us refer to as a good sleep it is the time of total forgetfulness of our name and our form, of all the other ideas, goals and worries which we seem to take as real during the time of being awake or of sorting out during dream time. In fact almost everyone in the world and today there are thousands of medicines for this purpose (including drugs and alcohol) which every individual longs for, in order to have this sound sleep whereby he may forget the person called "I" with all its attributes, thoughts and desires.

It is indeed a strange paradox that the very entity which we

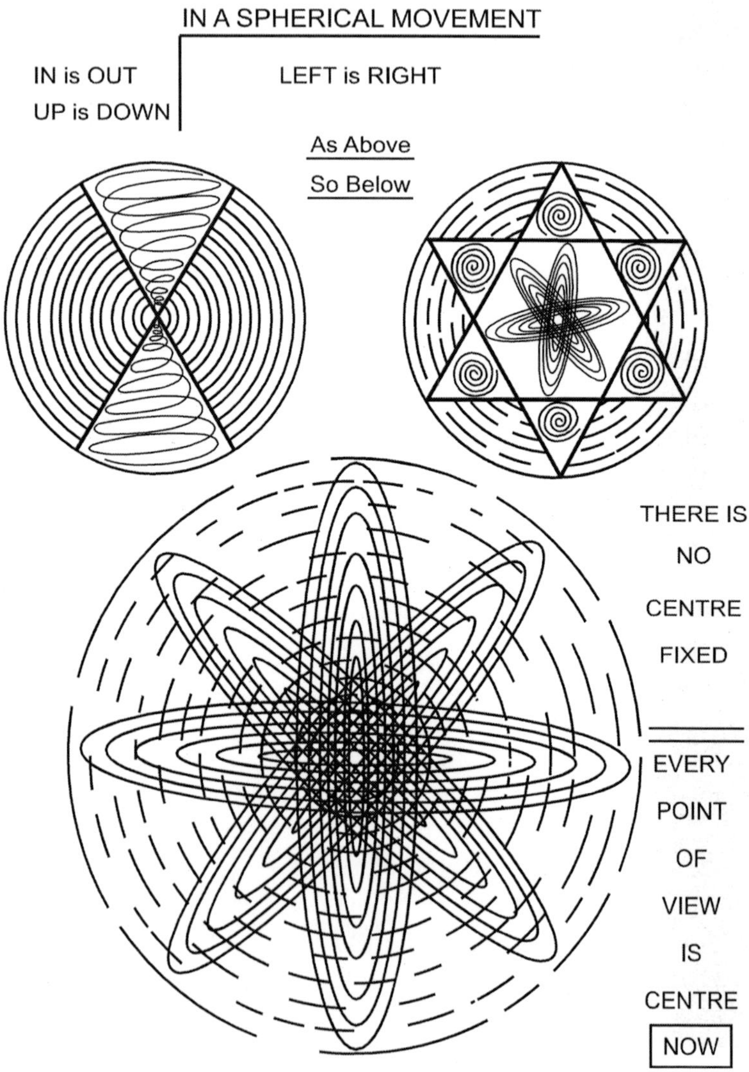

fig. 9.1: Spherical movement

Explanation to *fig.* 9.1

If one by contemplation discrimination, by enquiry looks into this the domination of linear mind, it's abstract nature, then only one may notice that this world, the planetary, galaxies and all move in a spherical total movement. Actually the universe is not going anywhere, it just goes round and round, it is a cyclical movement spiralling movement. However, in linear time, one moves from to here to there back and forth, especially mentally, in language, in order to achieve to get somewhere mentally psychologically in order to get name, fame, success, approval, attention. This is all in the nature of a conditional self. It comes, beginning from childhood, thus are there comparisons and measurements, etc. that this social self is never feels contented, basically psychologically that one is not alright one is not ok. In this relative world comparisons are an ongoing process especially creating as in the already notions existing, there are benchmarks situationally and contextually benchmark within one's head, that little professor J. Gurdieff, judging evaluating constantly. It does not allow one to accept and acknowledge one's self. It's the false linear mind of abstraction that overwhelms the perspective. It does not allow the acknowledgement of the NOW.

On the other hand, in a sphere or spherical movement, there is no up or down, there is no centre fixed, it changes according to the context, every point of view (often under social agreement) becomes the centre of Now. This is not only the outer layers but every aspect of the content functions within the some movement rotating nature of the movement of spheres, like musical spheres. Here there is no fixed left and right, nothing above or below. As above so below up is down and in is out and *vice-a-versa* and so on. Not being aware of the movement which is the earth itself, humankind is out of order, there is disorder in the human brain, he/she is not flowing with the movement. He/she is flowing against the flow, say, one is in the river going upstream for a long time and not suceeding. Against the flow and in linear time it imagines "one day" he/she will succeed. This is chasing a mirage of tomorrow and tomorrow!

take to be so real and by it have created a tremendous civilization, this unit of existence is what each one of us wants to magically disappear out of existence somehow, in order to attain a certain peace of mind. This is one of the paradoxes of the existence which can be dealt with only at the level of discovering the nature of consciousness. A point to ponder for every human being with a deep quality of awareness is, how is it that that which we take to be real, we want to forget completely? Perhaps the deeper psyche does know the false nature of this "I" and wishes to forget its existence in order to discover its own true state. It is the false entity which creates all the misery, suffering and pain. And the first step is to be aware of the false — "to see the truth in the false" — in order to be truly alive and in a fundamental sense to be a human being — a very conscious one. Otherwise, the neurotic-contradictory functioning continues; this pulls in two directions, i.e. the creation of the "I" and the need to forget it. This neurotic instrument cannot create peace and harmony. This paradox is the cause of conflict and tension, albeit not from the viewpoint of *what is, the actual.* It is in this enquiry of "who am I?" which has been stated very simply, we may briefly highlight some of the basic ideas as follows:

1. The "I" which refers to the body is made up of all the elements that exist on earth, as well as the total functioning of the universe that becomes the matrix of its existence. The body itself is the matrix and not outside of it. This is to say the viewer is in the picture though he often imagines seeing the picture outside of himself. Thus, he is both the effect, and affects the picture all around him.

2. At the mental level the self-conscious person is in the context of thoughts which arise in him; these are the effects of not only social conditioning but all collective memories, or the memory pool within which mankind has evolved through the ages. But this is not only in the sense of superficial thoughts which make up for these mental aggregates, of what is called the "I", since this label of thought is the effect of the deeper — what are called the unconscious layers — that one is not aware of. In effect, the superficial layers of the personal self, like the waves on the ocean are the result of the unconscious ocean of memories and knowledge, or what is called the stuff of consciousness which is the cause

of the surface movements. In a discussion of the person there is no actual "conscious self" and an "unconsciousness" since it is all one state of unconsciousness when one is "asleep", but when "awake", it is all consciousness. But simply by the fact of creating such operational divisions, these separate categories do not split this "one movement of consciousness", if we may call it that — provided one is aware of it. This is quite like the statement about the body which is an unconscious mental statement, by being unaware of the dimensions considered earlier, to be outside the picture. One might correctly state it in the reverse, that it is all consciousness.

3. Purely in terms of verifiability through even our everyday awareness and attention, when a little time is devoted to examine it, even what we call "myself" as the body or thought, its knowledge so to speak empirically speaking, is very meagre indeed compared to what we assume to know or claim with such certainty about what is this "I" or "myself". This is in the context of the inability to see it in an "objective" sense by our sensory organs, such as the eyes, or ears or even the body and all the functioning which takes place on its own, quite naturally, though we would like to believe as if we can see it or have any control of the senses and their functioning. In fact, both in the waking period and in the dream time we cannot see ourselves, nor control whatever takes place, broadly speaking. In a way, dream time is the continuum of the waking activities, which the brain tries to sort out by putting the physical body to sleep as these require rest through peace and harmony since most of the waking time of "I" is an existence of conflict and in duality that creates chaos and disorder in the brain cells. In the so-called activity of the person or self-consciousness little time is devoted to an acute awareness or observation. Thus, the same functions are carried out during sleep in peace and harmony, without the "I" interfering. The mechanism puts the "I" to sleep. It requires, even in dreams, to recuperate and conserve and restore the energy lost in a conflict of the false

"I". It may be noted that without choice and little knowledge directly of one's body one claims its ownership, but which one hesitates to say the same about the universe, why? That is, all the physiological functions happen naturally without "my" knowing, or doing; for example, breathing which becomes irregular if "I" try to breathe voluntarily and "self-consciously". Try it!

4. It is noted by everyone in daily life that sleep with this dream activity (while it is necessary as a clearing house of chaos and disorder) does not give a kind of rest to the mind and body unless there is a period of deep sleep when there are no dreams whatsoever. Not only that but one is completely oblivious of the body, activities of the mind and therefore of the name, label and all the so-called worries and complexities with which one has grappled the day long. When one wakes up from this kind of a sleep, there is a certain freshness once again and a feeling of rest and harmony in order to face the waking state again. Of course, as the mind wakes up thought activity and the self-conscious "I" is reactivated and while it recalls the sound sleep of the previous stored up memories and attributes which become the core of the existence of this person, the "I" looms large all over again.

5. The moments of sound sleep — or no thought state — are also occasionally experienced in another sense, say, by chance or at random during the waking state whenever one faces some sudden situation of shock which is a tragic situation or a beautiful experience. What happens is, that, in this suddenness of a shock situation the events for a split second or the moment is incomprehensible for thought or that conscious level which may not at that instance recollect from its memory pool any explanation. This is when people use the expression the "mind stopped" or some such statement which implies that all the processes and activities of explanations, judgements, conclusions are not available. It is a kind of disappearance of the "I" when there

is an awareness and an observation without any observer or the self-conscious activity which is called the "I". These moments are soon translated by thought, as this is its nature, habit and pattern. Yet these moments — as one recalls — also become memorable moments of an experience of states which one says are inexpressible, even ineffable, and "beyond the mind". It is a kind of total forgetfulness of the superficial activity when one gets in touch with fundamental layers of not mere existence, but "beingness"! These are actually states which we all know that give us a feeling of aliveness, though the "I" dies for that moment. It is only later on when thought creates a fear once again of its own death; that we imagine any such states where the "I" will disappear and when we say "what will happen to me?" Obviously nothing, for one is alive during such moments consciously without any choice, without any motivation, without any idea of the consequences and desire for results, that is, in these rare moments, there is no motivation, there are no fears of reward or punishment, no memories of happiness or regrets or resentments and all of the paraphernalia. In all the consciousness of the stuff of it that the "I" is made up, all that disappears; yet, awareness remains, a different impersonal consciousness remains, a kind of beauty and joy remains. It is like the organism which is consciousness itself, is experiencing itself which is the universe as a whole and there is neither an experiencer nor the experienced. It is only an expression of these states, when translated into an imperfect and imprecise language and expression, and manifestation being in terms of classifications and categories. This event for the sake of our convenience, or let us say the convenience of the existence of the false self; the experiencer, the experienced and experiencing categories are created. We all know that this convenience is soon taken to be the actual and even as a permanent state. It is clear that every human being has experienced these moments. Yet since these take place at random or accidentally, especially in the modern world, it is taken to be a mystic or supernatural phenomenon with which normally one claims not to have any intrinsic relationship. This is very far from the truth and is a denial of one's own experience, and one's own being, to the quality of life. It means that one has surrendered to unconscious conditioning, surrendered to a robot-like existence that is governed by a negative and destructive form of energy. It is a partial and fragmentary kind of living.

The "I" is, at the self-conscious level, a partial and fragmented mirage-like creation. This being so it attempts through all these false concepts and notions to complete itself in various ways that already exist in society or are created by us in our professions and in our relationships to seek such completions. But the game of this false "I" is to seek this completion absolutely and yet never really to be completed. For one thing, if it is complete then it means the disappearance of the false entity, since wholeness is beingness and that does not require any of the false attributes. For another , the false "I" tries to complete itself since it is a thing (as with other things, meaning thought) through concepts of status or emotions and relationships by various conceptual roles, and emotional passions labelled as love, not only with the opposite sex, but with parents, children, etc. All such completions are always ephemeral and shortlived, for when the mind seeks completion, happiness and satisfaction in the external world it is simply not possible. It is a blind man leading another blind man, as if the putting together of all the externals will bring light to their eyes. Belief systems, conclusions and concepts are blind as far as the quest for peace and harmony is concerned. A fragmented entity cannot simply create wholeness in this manner (Krishnamurti 1982).

6. It is in this deluded state that every human being or civilization itself is seeking those rare moments of feelings of peace, joy and happiness which are within the experience of each of us and are in our capacity or potentiality so, completely. This awareness is part of our existence or our

beingness. Yet, given the system in which we live, we think that by "doing" and by "having" we shall be able to achieve this state of beingness. In this reverse order we continuously keep "doing" or "acquiring" and continue with thoughts and things. This is the elaboration of the moment of simply being. Little do we realize that the existence of the self-conscious "I" itself with its attributes of achievement, of receding utopias, is a perpetual movement of the mind that will never be complete, although it appears almost as if it is complete, or very shortlived and momentary. We may say that desire or fear which is in the stream of consciousness itself manifests in the form, a body, and the consequent aggregates in the mind as the self-conscious "I" which plays this game continuously. It continues because it is addicted to dissatisfaction, pain and misery; unless that exists, there will be no thought movement, since then only it takes on a totally opposite statement of "not wanting pain and misery".

7. In this context, whatever or wherever one is, the mind is seldom "with it" at the moment, since it always wants to be elsewhere by conceptualizing and categorizing the experience. The going from here to thereby creating ideas, images of what is to be achieved as abstractions, takes one away from the experience except perhaps sometimes. Thus, there is both the inability to reach the utopia, to be absorbed in that "now" state "with whatever is". This is what causes frustration and desperation. The avoidance of "here and now" is the cause of immense pain and suffering; it is due to the continuous movement of duality. Even if the pain is physical, its agony or suffering is a mental statement, due to its conceptualization of the images and concepts. This is the self-conscious "I" which has created the immense memories of hurts, pain and pleasures. These, it wants to repeat in a lazy, mechanical manner — unconsciously. This is an addiction of a part of the brain, as a sensory organ that seeks constant gratification through pleasure–pain movement — a mental game now — resisting being one's self.

8. Mechanical thought — as we have discussed it in this work — is basically lazy and its activities therefore become inactivity, for, it neither wants consciousness to be foremost nor watchful awareness. If it did, it implies "true living" and what may be termed as real action. What we "normally" call intense activity and "action", i.e. of "I" or thought, is therefore total "inaction". This is in the sense that all levels of results do not create a feeling, for long, of completion and satisfaction. Unconscious mechanical activity, for whatever its material worth, has in all these thousands of years not produced the proclaimed objective of peace and harmony for human civilization. These lofty ideals instead have led to one crisis after another, true to its nature since thought thrives on pain and misery and situations of crisis. For, otherwise, it would disappear as an entity. But by keeping experience in abeyance, it maintains itself. True experiencing, which is aliveness, is known to all from one's own knowledge directly, even at the most "mundane" level. It is the "real" thing that is "sacred", truly "religious". But due to social conditioning what we call "reality" is mainly conceptual, measurable (one of the root word of *maya* means, to measure) and comparable. It is not experiential but illusory, for, its existence is dependent and momentary. So, "action" and "reality" — normally that we know of — are actually "inaction" and "unreal" if we dwell for a moment to inquire to contemplate, to stand and stare. Then is sensed a quality of beingness named differently and includes variously worded experiential attributes such as awareness, insight, intelligence and attention. This is inherent in all of us, which becomes crucial if we want with 100 per cent intentions to get human civilization back on the rails once again.

   It is a quality of choiceless observation of the body and mind which may be termed as non-action or passive action albeit of a very high intensity. It is a kind of inexpressible action which brings one back to be the controller of the vehicle of thought and the body rather than being "at effect" or out-of-control, living conditionally and unconsciously. One has to be aware of this lopsided understanding, even at the thought level, because without this awareness, arises conflict. There is this already in existence awareness because "who we are" is already the being, our existence is beingness. In other words, the "I" is derived from that beingness itself. Beingness expresses itself in this form of fundamental existence. It is already there, full and complete even if it is in the form of the limited "I" which we mistakenly take to be a solid enduring entity. But beingness is one's ability, this is "what we always are", i.e. who "I" am is this beingness within which exist all creatures. Consciousness itself is expressing itself in various material forms. We are not who "we think we are" to be conceptually (Muktananda 1978). Thinker, thinking and thought are subsystems of the whole. Let us take a very simple example of a dancer, or a musician, or an artist who "creates". One becomes immediately aware of such persons who dance, or sing, "with their being", i.e. they are in contact with another deeper source of consciousness that expresses their beingness through and in that media. This is why it clicks with one's own consciousness, or quality of existence. This is the difference between a good dancer of this calibre and one artist who may know all the intricacies and mechanism of dance, music or painting, yet is unaware of his or her own being. This is easily seen in what may be called accomplished technically or mechanically well done performance but with the "soul" missing. This is to say that the quality of beingness is primary for "doing" and "having", not vice versa.

9. Beingness is our nature which is complete and whole; always satisfied and fulfilled (Pearce 1981). Coming from this state the activities of "doing" and "having" assume significance for these are not now self-motivated from a self-centred "I". In the total framework, daily life becomes an expression of joy, moment to moment in all of one's existence. Even negative qualitie — fear, anger and greed — disappear since these in a misdirected manner are seeking the same completion or fulfilment, or for a lack of the same. This

awareness naturally — which exists beyond the notions of space and time — expresses itself as peace and harmony. There is a kind of intelligence (meaning reading in-between the lines) which then begins to express itself through the vehicles of the body and mind. It should thus be clear that the "I" is neither the mind nor the body. "I" thus becomes a larger entity or a state of existence in which exist body and mind, or, one may even say there is only one body and one mind and only one "I". It is like the metaphor of the sun and its various reflections in different vessels wherein it is reflected. But because of the veils of mental illusions and the movement of water it is imagined that there are separate existences and many "I"s (Ramakrishna 1980). This is the Universal Self, as has been called in many of the ancient texts. We may briefly now turn to an area that takes us into the dimensions of the nature of birth and death, so far unnecessarily mystified by man. Beingness is man's existence; which he has not to find or achieve. He has just to remember (re-member means to put together), i.e. he has to wake up from the deep slumber into which he has fallen from times immemorial. A dismembered self has to be re-membered again, that is all!

10

The Pole of Birth and Death

In terms of the pole of dualities, just as pleasure and pain which go together like two sides of a coin, similar is the case of birth and death — these are parts of the same continuum. Therefore, any discussion of death can only take place in the context of birth. Without which it becomes an empty debate of words or a very one-sided discussion about death; that is, rather than an enquiry it becomes a topic arising out of fear and anxiety, the need for physical longevity, etc. In the normal course of our lives when we speak about birth and death we are really speaking about the body, i.e. as we have noted earlier the reference of the "I" — this self-conscious person — is a reference to one or another body directly; or its mental projections with larger and larger social groups or ideas about them. Thus, when we talk about death we mean that life or consciousness or that activity which gave that physical body aliveness or movement does not exist any longer. Again, when we talk about "I" was born or of birth, it is a reference to one's body and the parentage, or that is to say, a reference to the fertilization of an ovum, and into the outer world of a body in a given sociocultural set-up. Consequently, whatever else may be any other kind of discussion about birth–death we may get into from the philosophical viewpoint, in everyday life any talk of birth or death, or coming or going, is a reference to the appearance and disappearance of a bodily human frame. But this is also true for all other so-called "living" creatures if not the inanimate — "non-living" — ones to which we do not directly relate and hence do not apply this terminology; in fact, even plants are not "alive" for many people.

In the context of all that has been stated earlier, we could do well to reflect on the question "who was born?" or a statement like "I was born". Now we know that from the time the ovum was fertilized we are prone to call it "I", and the name with which "I" identifies with its body is to be "myself". If this is so, the "I" to which "I" am referring as the bodily person had little choice, i.e. in the body for its beginning not only depends upon the parents but also on the entire ancestry to which we have referred to already in the previous chapters. It is thus that the body emerges into the outer world through the agency of the mother. Along with this are the socio-psychological dimensions of the emergence (whatever its context as many modern psychologists have deeply gone into), into the name with which "I" identify. This is given not by my choice but a consequence of the sociocultural context which carries within it once again the entire pool of traditions and knowledge of not only my own society but that of the vast existence of humankind itself. All the attributes and characteristics, however, become limited by the conditioning, whereby is formulated into what is called the person, his name or "I", that checks, creates and regulates the shape of thought forms. Once again these thoughts, with which one identifies so easily, also come and go without any wilful choice or control in terms of either a beginning or an ending. In passing one may recall the fact that every child is conditioned into identifying itself with the name given. For example, while learning how to write, one reinforces this identification by writing one's name repeatedly as if the child were not sure about its identity and yet believes that since its parents say so it must be so. This, in other words, is what is called the formation of the personality that in due course becomes a hardened identity, a perpetual ego. Any child by itself is basically quite free of the categories and distinctions which grown-ups make. Often, this goes to the extent that a child does not distinguish between a dangerous animal and others. Even the development of taste buds is gradually conditioned by culture; and so is the case of all sensory perceptions that, so far, broadly speaking perhaps, perceive everything for *what is* clearly.

At any rate, it is only subsequent to the formation of such psychosomatic identity that one speaks of having been born, for, seldom does anyone consciously know either one's self or one's parents at birth. In a sense my existence today is the only proof that I must have been born as a body, and all the associated events and timings in this regard that I received only as information — not experience relived — from my parents, or in the social context. However, often, at moments, doubts about the accuracy of even this information also arise in one's mind.

If the question about the birth of the body is so unclear, the question about who was born is much more difficult. It involves asking a question about what was "I" before the body took form. Or, was there an "I", as a person, before the body was born? The latter is difficult to answer since the "I" or the person with which one identifies today was given a name, long after its appearance into the external world. Since this person is a social identity, was there any specific individual, or particularized social context before the body was born? If the person is taken to be an aggregate of his social conditioning and thought — an ideational form — it seems unlikely to be in existence before the form took shape. If this bodily existence is eliminated, then what may be considered to be in existence are the various ideas or thought-forms — a stream of consciousness — or some kind of "non-physical" — in the sense of the gross body form, potentialities. These perhaps may be called a subtle level or mental plane or body; perhaps this "intangible" (implicate or unmanifest) form condenses itself from one level of energy into a "tangible" (explicate or manifest) body form which is subsequently given a name and all the other attributes to become a person. These explanations of divisions are stated from a relative, personal or dualistic viewpoint — as an operational hypothesis.

Some kind of existence prior to birth at other "impersonal" levels logically becomes possible in terms of what has been stated above. This is the existence of energy form, or what may be called consciousness, without going into a semantic and terminological debate. The argument against this may be that it is not necessary to enunciate some extra "physical" dimension, since the birth of the physical organism is tied up to the rest of the physical world — the existential and the evolutionary levels. But if we carry this argument to its logical limits, the question arises as what existed before the first form of matter took birth? Then, in this dichotomy of the physical and the non-physical (both these terms are operational, for the very term "physical" implies the existence of its opposite, that is, not as confrontation but as continuum of one energy or one consciousness in this sense of a unitary holistic notion) once again the same dilemma faces one; that is, what condensed itself either in terms of evolutionary beginnings when we presume something happened at the first time, or even if we do not, seeing it in terms of an evolutionary perspective? Thus, if it is an ongoing process, what energy is there or what is that so-called stuff which gives rise to bodily forms? At the moment we are not worrying about the terminology except in being aware of the fact of the process of what is called the birth of the body which assumes logically that there was something earlier to that event, even if it was not the person.

For the moment let us leave this line of argument and look at it from another viewpoint; I am aware of my body, i.e. there is primordial consciousness — not self-consciousness though it is part of consciousness as well — and therefore I do know the existence of what I label "my body". Let us call this a mental notion of the body or of the person, but even here there has to be a consciousness at the mental level in order to be aware of my body and of everything else around me. Awareness and consciousness, which we feel as a characteristic of human existence, become a primary basis for the knowledge of the body, the name and the form. If there is no consciousness, there will be no mental formations and no knowledge of the body will exist. In such consciousness, it is the awareness of what one calls the past, the future and the present. Even if these are mere abstract notions and concepts, the essential nature is one of being conscious; or, having consciousness becomes the ground of existence. Thus, consciousness is primordial (say the Self or *I*), and then comes if one may state that consciousness as "I" comes into existence in a broader sense (say, *I am*); and, then only all the other ideas of thoughts or bodily existences and all the paraphernalia with which we are so concerned (say, *I am* so and so, etc., both as a process and as an identity). If consciousness is not only fundamental prerequisite but an attribute of the body, can we not say that it is consciousness which assumes these various forms, or that these forms are consciousness? But consciousness is still consciousness albeit in different shapes and forms in terms of our dual categories of expressions. Manifestation is a dimension of differentiation, of dualities but the vehicle of consciousness is consciousness itself. It is like my attributes and expressions are myself and my qualities and devoid of these qualities, there would be no me as such. This is like seeing the rays of the sun, for without the rays there would be no sun. There is no separation as such. For example, a statement like "I am eating", means consciousness as "I" (as Self) comes into existence *am* (a psychosomatic form), becomes a process of *eating* (or identifies with a name, label, etc.), i.e. I as Self is eating in an existential–experiential moment of *now*, moment to moment, but not as an abstract conceptual existence.

Thus either we say that bodies exist in consciousness or bodies are consciousness, but not that "I" (the ego sense) has consciousness as if the "I" came first and then consciousness. It is therefore the entire consciousness viewed from the viewpoint which is expressing itself in various forms. From another angle — and which we may call the evolutionary one — I am made up of all the elements around me and continue to do so by absorbing or eating all the other natural elements around me; also, all the elements of which the earth is made up are in me. I am then a product of and the outgrowth of the earth which is consciousness; then, the same consciousness must exist — in all the elements as well as the earth itself which in a true sense becomes now mother earth. The earth then becomes consciousness itself, for if it was not so, I or all the other forms that are products or children of mother earth, so to speak, would have no consciousness. If the earth is consciousness, then it is itself a part of the system of all the other universal elements present in the one universe with which it is connected and with which I am connected. In this sense, the universe as a physical form is the expression of Universal Consciousness. These expressions of the myriad forms are the way it expresses itself or manifests itself. The division between the "manifest" and the "unmanifest" once again stems from duality or a limited focus, for, finally it is one and the same thing, i.e. Universal Consciousness. Division and debate only take place when separate entities at the purely physical or social level see their existence in a partial or fragmentary context, not within the totality or wholeness. It is in this sense that the so-called paths, each being Universal Consciousness, are whole, else total. Each, like a grain of sand or a drop of water, is complete and whole in its essence and is part of what we may call a perfect system and is perfect in its essential nature, out of time and space concepts, eternally or in the eternal moments of *now*.

Following the logic even in an evolutionary sense — or the Big Bang theory of contemporary astro-physicists — in the beginning whatever took form in the shape of matter has a point or what may be called a *bindu;* in it existed all the potentialities for unless this was the case logically nothing else would appear or happen the way it is happening quite naturally and spontaneously. It manifests itself in that form wherein the seed also exists at the same time. In other words the macrocosm is in the microcosm and vice versa which the ancient seers saw long ago. The tree is in the seed and the seed in the tree. They also said or saw all this because the essence of this knowledge exists in every form since every form is Universal Consciousness. But one knows this, when the ground is fertile for the seed to grow or that energy to become self-evident. This means giving up the erroneous notions or mental agitations of the limited self-conscious person which obscures — like the cloud in the sky — the existence of the eternal sun. Does not, when the mud is removed, the needle buried in the ground, it become naturally one or united with the magnet! The other analogy is the one about the existence of light which no one, not even the scientists, has ever seen. Yet, each one of us knows that there is light for whatever we see around is the effect of light both metaphorically and literally. The eye does not see by itself but it sees because of light or shall we say it is light that sees itself, or its manifestations and effects. In other words we may say it is Universal Consciousness that sees and interacts through various forms which are its own creations (*fig.* 10.1).

In this elementary discussion of the problem of birth we notice that Universal Consciousness is our very nature, i.e. of who we

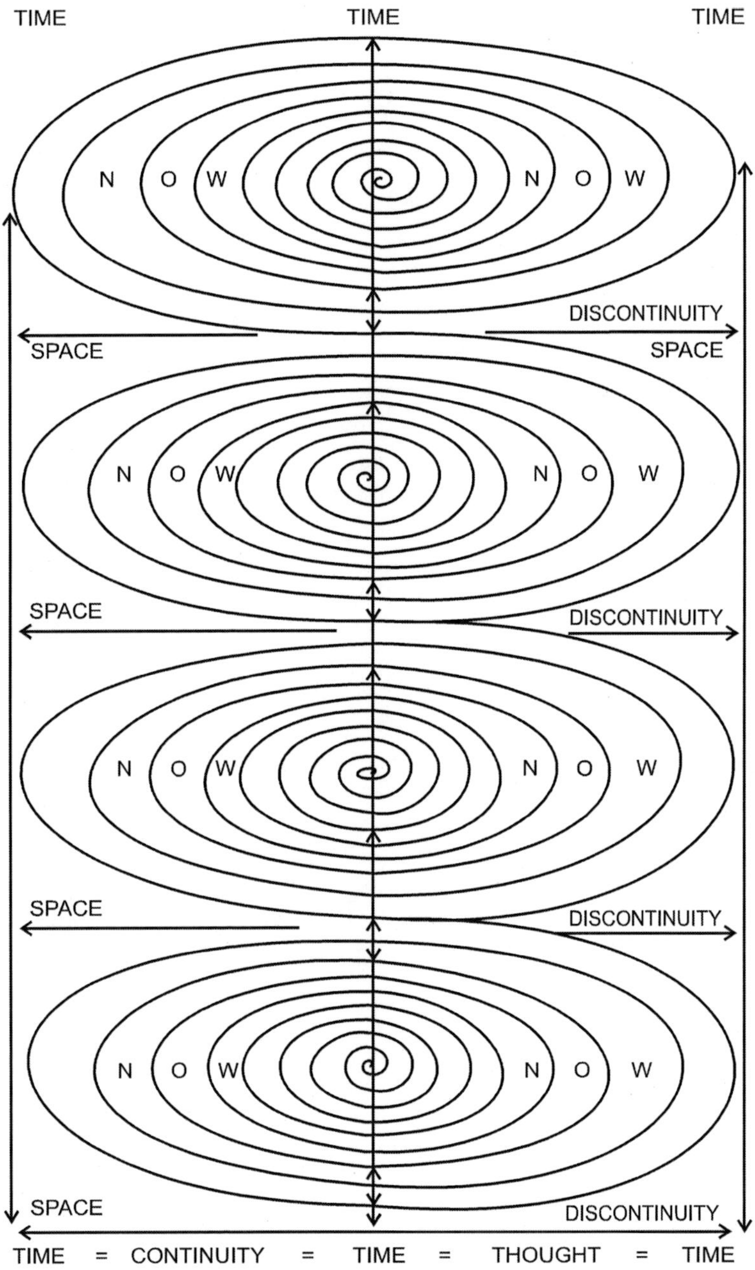

fig. 10.1: Thought is time

Explanation to *fig.* 10.1

As said earlier time is a conceptual construct and especially in the context of thought, its movement. This allows for, created by the concept of linear time, that there is a continuity, past, present, future, cause and effect. But these are abstract conceptual notions. However if one moves out of the notion of this conceptual ideas of phenomenal events, this subsystem produced by certain various cultural groups, then one may begin to get glimpse into a holistic universe, when the mind's chatter stops. In this context there are only moments of Now which occur as horizontal spherical movements within which all occurs. For instance, words and deeds move into this horizontal sphere yet not disappear, eventually these are vibrational movements, as there are no solid stuff, it is created by naming, labelling, the word especially being created by conditioning. This is true for modern left brain domination. Then there are a serious Now in this spherical vibrational universe, occurring in space function in this manner, going nowhere except that there transformations of energy with one "form" into another. It is like a caterpillar turns into a butterfly and so on. Contextually thought creates time, there is actually no time, contextually culturally conditioned.

Thus the universe is a discontinuous one, there is no "real" continuity except in the language words and thought. Words are actually sound vibrations and impact the receiver and sender when spoken and hidden as energy when written and very much so in the realm of music. There are also musical spheres. There are no solid things at all, if one see from the viewpoint of Now, as of Here and Now, of Presence.

are. If so, what do we say about death? What we call death is the death of the body, but why does this become such a problem of agony and turmoil? We are all aware that the birth of the body was not in our hands and that as an organism it is more or less genetically determined when it shall come to an end. Not only that we see this kind, of our own ending, all around us in the human species but as men we are also responsible for the ending of other organisms for our own use; as well, we see it in nature, in the context of animals and plants or if one may even call the changing patterns of the inanimate objects, of the rivers and mountains which are gradually transformed from the inorganic to the organic. Thus in some timeless ways, there are continuities, that means that birth and death — eternal cycles — are constantly taking place and that all the physical forms at every moment not only on earth but in the universe of stars and galaxies are changing. Seeing this, why is there still such an agony and pain and anguish to what we call the death of the organism? The fact is that it is the separation into this false "I" or person from the universal nature of things that is the cause of pain and anguish. The person or "I", with its ideational attributes of thought which are conceptual in nature, forms so many castles in the air with regard to itself and its relationship that with reference to its own or other bodies it is unable to give up these dimensions. Thought being fragmentary, incomplete and therefore dependent on all the notions which it has created (and which we have dealt with earlier), fears its own extinction, its attachments or to memory of all the experience it has put together and formed these castles in the air. The focus is wrongly on the body, although the body is used for the repetition of sensory pleasures including repetition of painful experiences in the crises on which it thrives. This entire illusory set-up of a dream world is threatened once again, in an imaginary way. This is imaginary because the passing away of another body is the ending of that organism, and most of us in actuality also do not really care for our own bodies or of other human bodies, not to speak of animals which we destroy all the time. There is therefore a falseness in these attitudes. At this level and at the level of thought which continuously uses, exploits and corrupts in its need for power and authority; that reinforces its existence within the person or "I" howsoever large the number of bodies that may be included in the concept of the "I".

Thought moves at this ideational level and the person is thus an idea or image attached to all the other images. So the death of another body is my own image and its existence because of the attachment of pleasure and pain which I was deriving through this other one. Pain and agony are not the loss or going away of another person but the loss of my own pain or pleasure that I was utilizing through that person. It is this notion of "I" and "mine", which is possessive in its very fundamental nature since it is not an independent but a dependent entity, a fragment trying to hold itself together by another person and idea. The movement of thought and its incessant chatter is this sort of set-up. It is far and away from actual experience and therefore lives in the world of make-believe. Death in actuality would really mean the termination of all this stream (the horizontal, it may be called, of the linear mind) of consciousness of the person or false identity of the "I" and all its attributes of fear, anxiety, pleasure and pain, its loneliness and so on. Moving beyond this cycle and the ending of duality of movement of thought as a separate entity is actually dying or death. This stream of consciousness, not the Universal Consciousness (the vertical, we may call it of the holistic mind) or supreme intelligence which we have referred to earlier, obviously exists before and after the birth and death of a body. The death of the body is therefore not really the death of that stream of consciousness which continues to flow ever increasingly since fear and anxiety and all the other negative dimensions continue to exist at that non-tangible level to continuously manifest itself. This stream of consciousness is the entire game of thought and thought-forms which have taken control of the instrument of the body for its own perpetuation. At its expense, the true flowering of Universal Consciousness, or the essence, is kept in abeyance. A movement out of this stream of consciousness through acute awareness or choiceless observation or what is called witness consciousness is the first step to go beyond what we call birth. It is dying to this entire contrary direction of movement that now emerges the essential "I" or the Self which is our true nature. The dying of the small "I" is the only way out to capture what may be called the true aliveness of life itself. This is what allows that oneness or the eternal source to function appropriately in all its forms. It is this one "I" that is the only subject reflected in all these smaller "I"s that now becomes the objects in which it operates according to its universal nature. The intellect, or thought itself, must understand these simple elementary processes of "understanding", if it is to move into that other dimension. This understanding is the first step that takes one naturally, or reveals one's essential nature by itself once the beginning has been made.

11

Creativity and Self-Expression

It must be obvious from the previous chapters that for any enquiry into creativity and self-expression, it is essential to examine the falseness or truth of the given search. So, since it is by a seeker or pursuer, who or what is the seeker? Basically, in the normal course of life and this "normal" is not the natural, any discussion of creativity or self-expession has a reference to the person, or the self. Perhaps, the distinction between the seeker and the sought is a false one. Is there a "self and others"? (Malik, 1986). Normally, the self in this case is defined as the person, one who has a self-image, created by social conditions. In turn, it projects and identifies itself with other persons and other non-human existence. It does so especially because of the various generalized and abstract sociocultural concepts such as family, society, nation and so on within which one lives. There is no individual existence without relationships, be it with nature or humans; whether this relationship exists in the person's mind or outside one's self, he or she cannot exist without relating.

The word "person", a synonym for self, means mask (Latin derivative — *personal*), i.e. the person or personality is a role-playing entity. Each one of us is conditioned to play a sociocultural role or roles from the word go — from birth — within a givenness of an "action–reaction" system. There is no choice in this physio-psychosocial set-up the person is born within or under. But soon in performing one or many of these conditioned roles, one begins to believe or impart an intrinsic reality to the roles or the dominant self-image one is playing that with which the person identifies most closely. Most of the time one does believe in its intrinsic reality, with a will and intention "to do" or "I am the doer".

But deep doubts arise, when the person becomes dissatisfied; especially when things do not go one's way. In various ways, one begins to seek knowledge, happiness and the like. One attempts to be whole. Yet, the person is seldom content. Why? Because an image cannot become the substance, or whole, since by its very nature the mask is incomplete, a cover-up. It being nothing but the result of having various conditioned roles. This experiencing structure by its very nature is one of incompleteness. This shadow of an entity is the cause of the eternal problem of the psychological state of loneliness, the restless soul, etc. The very creation of the problem and seeking a solution is the case of its perpetuation, so to maintain the momentum. Loneliness or separation is inherent in this identity of an incomplete, contradictory and limited state of existence. The very nature of the person or the ego is to create the notion of "separation", "alienation" albeit suitably and subtly covered.

Next in order to be free, it creates the problem of attachment–detachment, bondage–freedom, limitedness–liberation and so on. The endless debate is what the ego feeds on, and with which mankind has struggled for eons, hoping and waiting. To be free the person thus seeks a wider identity with larger and larger groups, newer abstractions, celestial beings, gods; all very subtle games. Nevertheless, all these attempts create even further insecurity. Its true nature is comfortably obliterated. Of course, the insecure, uncertain nature of this entity, this imaginary centre — the person — stays the same, only the circumference increases. How and who will find the solution? The more these attempts, the more the agitation and despair. In the stream of consciousness the signs of a great lack of integral relationship within one's self become wider, its projections become the society at large and which itself functions within the great illusion. By now, any awareness of this conditioning — the falseness — within a limited set of notions, images, concepts, etc. is totally blocked out. No light enters the prison which is considered real, home, and intricately decorated as if it will lead one on to the road to freedom. It is the old snake–dragon symbolism—eating the tail of another—endlessly! As long as the false notion of a separate intrinsic "real" personal existence is not realized (as insight or as vision), knowing that the personality and social conditions are one and the same thing, the struggle and effort for knowledge and happiness along with all of the futility and despair subsumed under it become an endless cycle. The more the belief of one's self to be living in isolation, as islands of self-enclosures, the receding mirage, elusive-phenomenon, continues to cover up, and/or pursues freedom. A natural corollary to this, despite temporary satisfactions, is the feeling — sooner or later surfaces — of being either unrelated or of having the feeling of incompleteness, of unsatisfactory relationships, or dissatisfaction in one's state of existence in whatever one does; including the so-called "creative" efforts, seeking knowledge and so on. The various objectives, the need for wanting to achieve are basically escapes — means of avoidance — from this fundamental conflict or neurosis of the mind. The obvious outlets are to seek social recognition and power even altruistically or spiritually, or it is in terms of food, sex, politics, fame, etc. albeit in very sophisticated ways now.

Thus, the pursuer in short is not what it is thought of; it is unclear, or even non-existent. If so, what can it pursue by way of knowledge, creativity or happiness? The creation of a separateness of the person or self, impinges upon the creation of the others, which includes goals and objectives to be achieved, desired, wanted; even such noble truths as knowledge or inner joy. But for whom, and for what? What is the context? The question being false, the solutions are endless, without answers. In this way, there is an entire universe of debates, and the illusion gets to be perpetuated. To give an example, one of the ways to achieve wholeness is reflected in the entire enterprise of interdiscipline, i.e. trying to create integration. But this only extends the notion of separateness, since our lives are governed by the notion of duality, or of dichotomy. It is further reflected in such notions as autonomy vs wholeness, science or art vs society, identity vs alienation, domination vs subordination, you vs me, conflict vs consensus and so on. Can an unintegrated, partial, fragmentary self or society become whole or integrated? These various notions are value-orientations that have become a basic — in the sense of uninvestigated or covert assumptions — or integral parts of our lives, whether the context is industrial, urban, rural — in a developing or developed society.

This heritage is of a long-standing way of thinking, of our presuppositions of human existence, i.e. dualism is a part and parcel of one of the world views. It has become the dominant philosophy in this century. This is not to say that it does not represent a valid viewpoint in some ways — it has served its limited purpose. But it is no longer appropriate in the context of a changing world. What this dominating world view has done is that it has in the process submerged many other equally forceful (perhaps more appropriate) and even larger standing representations of reality. For instance, all polarizations may be seen as a continuum, i.e. it is a "you and me" universe. Again, such universal principles as feminineness and masculineness — whether it is called Śiva–Śakti or Ying–Yang today — may appear as "opposites" yet these are not in opposition. Neither is good or bad. Both simply are. They exist as complementarities within the whole. The complementarity of these parts is an intrinsic quality of this "whole", which is very necessary for a functioning harmonious universe. However, too much of one or the other principles upsets the balance, i.e. too much or too little of either is harmful. In this world view balance, harmony, proportion, cooperation are the important values that form the ground of *One's Being*. All are part of nature or cosmos (meaning order). A whole universe which includes all, and all "living and non-living" things exist as equals, as Beings. Therefore, the need for such concepts as the mastery over nature do not arise. Beings are already in harmony, in tune, and therefore with this realization a human being arrives as a Master, with this direct knowledge. This natural continuum is shared by all animate and inanimate, past, present and future in the *Now*. In short, all that "exists" or "not-exists" are complementary parts of *what is*, i.e. all are interacting in a continuous, on-going process.

Thus, the universe is a process, it is a whole of which you and I are a part, albeit a part from the human viewpoint, not from what is. We may view wholeness as existing in the parts, and that is why they are able to interact, interrelate, communicate and commune. The universe as a process may be considered conceptually as having one horizontal continuum of space, intersected by a vertical continuum of time whereby we locate for human purpose, all events (*fig*. 11.1).

The Western or "modern" world view emphasizes "things" and gives it an intrinsic reality. This limited view of reality — as things — the world in the twentieth century has borrowed overwhelmingly in the wake of industrialization; it has made civilized man to become "thing-minded" only. Much of our thinking is "thinging". Our concern has become one of identifying and arranging the symbols that represent the universe, far away from any experiential reality. The illusory attempts to improve, interrelate, create harmony through concepts, plans and institutions — all are continuing very vigorously. But the fundamental problems even of survival, remain the same despite the enormous availability of resources. Limited thinking — or thinging more appropriately — cannot achieve any significant results. Today, we would like to believe in having "advanced". Is this so? While primitive man used arrows as missiles, modern man uses nuclear warheads. While earlier a few were killed, now many millions are exterminated. The jump is mostly quantitative. Yet because of the impending total catastrophe, only a qualitative transformation is called for. The very nature of this crisis makes our century a crucial juncture of creation and destruction. Both the choices are available to us clearly. Evolutionarily speaking, either way is of little consequence, i.e. whether man survives or not. What matters is that the dynamism of life continues.

The personification of the universal spirit — or Self — appears in the context of the diversity of people, objects, even gods in the manifested process. But the universal force — the unseen — itself is not a thing. That is what "nothingness" means — "no-thing-ness", i.e. the void — both emptiness and fullness — shapeless, formless, nameless. In it are both Beingness and not-Beingness;

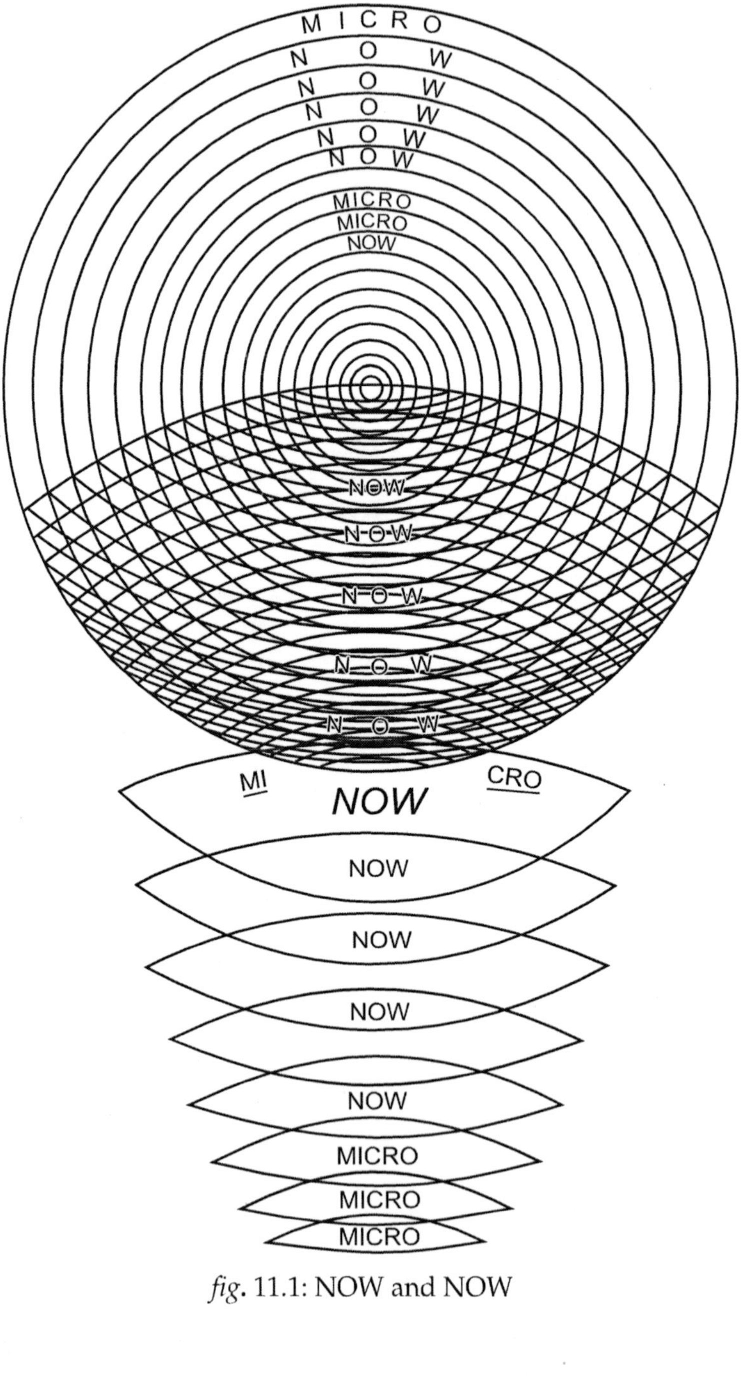

fig. 11.1: NOW and NOW

Explanation to *fig.* 11.1

In this spherical spiral movement, it is going no where. There are only the moments of Now that occur at the macro and micro level. This means those movements occur also say at both the body and mental level. And by having mental movements the cellular and micro level happens say whatever the mental level perspective is it impacts the motion of the cells. The body mind system is one, whole. This system becomes subsystem in the context of the larger systems which are then their subsystem is the context of larger system and so on. In other words finally it is all one system, everything connected to everything like using "things" or thought in our language for words. And thinking is thinging, these are not any two separate categories. Like me and thought is the same. The thinker is thought, is "me" an abstract socially constructed concept which through conditioning appears as real and solid.

It is well to remember their context of a total whole, not the separateness which thought has made out, actually a false concept of "reality". Not knowing this, one feels isolated, alienated and lost. This is the absence of relatedness or interrelatedness. One is definitely not an autonomous independent self. We, one has existence only as a relational self, related to all human, animals, plants all the elements, the earth, ocean, skies and planetary system and in the universe. So every part of the universe is the universe and everything occurs together, simultaneously. All separateness, uniqueness, is an absrtract concept, however uniqueness is the expression of the manifestation of the ONE, the universe appearing in different forms, from our viewpoint, not from the viewpoint of the universe. It is the same energy, ENERGY. It is like the often stated saying that there is only One Sun and is reflected in different vessels, but there is only One Sun. In face there is only ONE Energy system, call it Fullness or Void or Emptiness, from our perspective.

both existence and non-existence. All words, terms, expressions in any form, etc. are parts of the structure of cultural symbols that represent reality variously and, therefore, are approximations to truth. This is why the inclusion of everything in *That*; all of the so-called contradictions, the paradoxes, appear so only from the limited human viewpoint. By *itself it* is not so. Take the example of light; its effects are seen but itself we cannot see it. It creates the manifested expressions yet is uneffected — being itself limitless with no relation to the limited. In other words, the manifest becomes the unmanifest and the unmanifest the manifest. *That which is*, is beyond labels, it is unstructured. The box of a limited paradigm has to be dropped. The limited person cannot grasp the whole, until the little "I" disappears. The delusion of a separate self as something non-existent, this is the hardest to grasp. The wave is the "me" in the ocean of the Self which disappears when the ocean changes shape. The wave is the ocean itself. This me is indeed a mere sociocultural being — it is governed by genetic and cultural conditioning — since its behavioural patterns are determined by its identity with everybody around the me. At one level, me is the result of an "action–reaction", "cause–effect", "stimulus–response" system. But even here, the personality in fact is not separate because within it are contained all of the responses to all of the conditioning of the entire human consciousness, albeit manifested in a limited way by biological and cultural conditionings. There exists the possibility of being sensitive to this conditioning — the awareness of it. This is why there exists — the widely prevalent search by and within the personality, the me, to discover its true — real Self in various ways. While in this search of the limited me, for the unlimited and infinite is inevitably futile, nevertheless the masks fall away; one discovers there's nothing in the end, like peeling an onion. But in this process various creative expressions — among writers, painters, in music, science and whatever — are revealed at different times in various civilizations. But of course the me is not visible albeit great creative works are produced in the process.

Another common metaphor is that of a raindrop. This may be taken as the person who, clinging to the limits of the surface-tensions of the raindrop, experiences necessarily only that much, a personality of which it is so proud. But what happens if it loses its identity? This is an impossible situation, full of fear and anxiety. The lower mind, as me, keeps up its search of rational explanations, because it must maintain its surface-tension or personality. But when there is the losing or letting-go of — at times of accidents, or overwhelming sudden beauty — that fleeting illusive notion, then another dimension opens up. These moments are soon forgotten, or classed as unbelievable hallucinations. But within the heart of one's heart, the longing is for a return to that moment — now reified and therefore an impossibility in that sense. However, the realization comes in a direct manner, that the ocean or Self is what created the raindrop. The raindrop now is an expression of the Self. The person is both the limited and unlimited expressions of the ocean, because otherwise it is non-existent. The me is a part of the painting, a participant of a process, all occurring simultaneously, holistically and not in a linear fashion. One is no longer an alienated outsider. The *Beingness* now flowers within the person. It is a direct insight into reality, a return of the prodigal. Here is the realization that one was never away from home, that there was no going away, that there was no such thing as a separate person.

True Self-expression is thus an expression of wholeness — the oneness. All attempts — conscious or unconscious — are a groping towards *That*. The intrinsic need is to restore wholeness, the quality of life. Self-expression requires each of us to be sensitive on all fronts, i.e. not only to the profession or pursuit but a sensitivity of the eyes, ears, taste, smell, touch, thoughts; allowing a total functioning of the Being. Thus, being sensitive there comes forth a natural — spontaneous — responsibility for and of the universe (not in this sense of shame or guilt) for the "evils" of mankind; hunger, injustice, dirt, ugliness or whatever. This very acknowledgement is, therefore, an expression of this sensitivity.

This moment of self-realization or self-actualization reveals the truth that we are interrelated and totally responsible for all that happens in the world, including socially and humanly responsible to mankind in the wider sense of the world. Therefore all our authentic acts — all creativity — are an expression of *That*, that includes All. It comes from the basic truth that whatever we do, each one of us has a meaningful role in the expression of harmony and beauty, wholeness and virtue. The possibility exists in each one of us to make a vital difference, in our own way to make the world healthy/holy — once again. It comes from a knowing that there is only *That*. The raindrop knows it is what makes the mighty ocean, knowing it is the ocean to begin with, an intrinsic nature of ourselves, this source allows one to operate and function, i.e. to *express, do, have* and *function*. It is not as we believe, we *do, have* and *possess* in order to achieve a wholeness. A fragment cannot achieve wholeness unless it realizes its beingness, first. It is not that we accumulate knowledge (information), as things which get us to be creative. Creativity brings about knowledge. Each one of us has the innate nature to be creative, we were born like that. All creation is that — until social conditioning destroys it and then once again we wish to get back to the source, the innocence necessary for creation, which as children we have known.

Self-expression — not the self-conscious entity — and creativity (when coming from the true source) are always inspiring. They empower others and, in others reactivate the same source. That is why the state is nourishing. This does not mean that the individual is not unique (not in the sense of isolated, separated). Each one of us is both unique and the same. Paradoxically, while we are different, yet we are the same. This is much like all things that are different — yet, each is the expression of the same source — not better, worse, more or less; except when there is social agreement. The true individual may be considered unique only when he lives his life consciously, fully as a human being.

Thinking like this, one may be minus a function socially speaking, yet remain authentic. The creator and the created become a part of the entire activity of creating or creation, from moment to moment — in the eternal *now*. This may sound like all else, like being irresponsible, or lacking any sense of discipline. But the word "discipline" really means to learn, to create and to go into the unknown, the unthinkable. It is to live in uncertainty, insecurity; it is to live in a paradox. The creative processes is a paradox manifested. It becomes different, even contrary to the experience. In the illusion of life, these human expressions are reflections only of that reality, which is not describable (like life); not even verbalized and even symbolized. In other words, thinking about life is not life. Life is living it. Yet, in truth all of it is included

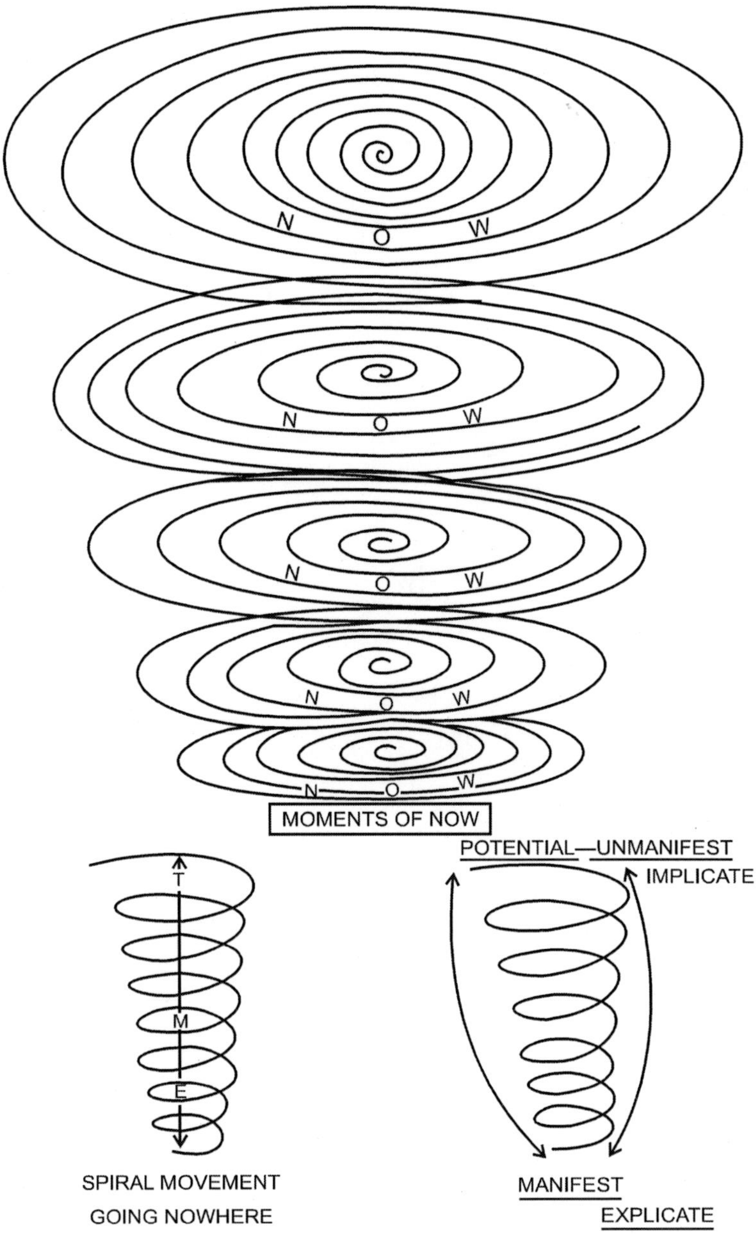

fig. 11.2: Implicate and explicate movement

Explanation to *fig.* 11.2

There are moments of Now, and each Now is a horizontal spherical rotating spiral movement going nowhere so to speak. It is at first the implicate order when unmanifest, it has all the potentials available. Then when it is manifested it is explicate order. While this movement spiral is going no where, the emergence of my thought becomes a barrier, and one has to see that this is only a subsystem confined by sociocultural context. It is well to remember that in this totality, this wholeness the conceptual and abstract notions of human beings is part and parcel of the universal movement. However in this process one is struck at the subsystem which is also changing yet one gets sucked into a fragment. It is like the entire society is fragmented, there is extreme specialization, it is like seeing the leaves and forgetting the trees. Or, it is when one is riding a bicycle going uphill one wheel gets loose and goes off down hill, one starts chasing it down hill and in this process forgets about the total bicycle. Moreover, in this modern days analytical age of this logical left brain, say if one wants examine a chair one believes that by first breaking the chair and examining each part one will one day put it together, forgetting that the chair is already whole and complete. Similarly, the universe is already One and whole and the microcosm and macrocosm is already One. The question to ask is why do we see it as separate and then trying to put it together. The separation is because of fragmented limited conceptual perspective of thought.

— nothing excluded. It is an expression of a higher truth. It is a process of changing forms of thought, and awareness, into other forms, none equivalent, yet all expressive aspects of an outer and inner reality. The process, like the universe itself, is inexhaustible and never-ending (*fig.* 11.2).

In this sense the abstract becomes the concrete beyond the logic of negation; negation of itself creates something else. It is a return to the metaphysics, and to which we referred earlier. It is not a way through a jumble of words, theories and theses that rationalize creativity and self-expression. But spontaneity is not the same as impulsive action; it is a doctrine of action, that is immediately appropriate, by instantaneous, unconscious reflexes to the situation without the need for thought. The true measure of creativity is its effortlessness, albeit the basic mastery of the technique is essential, almost as if creativity, nay, true creation is out of "nothingness".

The process of creation in operation is the same in all, though different in its expressions. But the individual becomes self-centred when he thinks he is autonomous, i.e. if he ignores the universal nature of his labour or if he speaks or pampers class or group interests in society. These "universals" cannot merely be claimed aloud; these have to be judged by the person in creative process by himself about his motivations, expectations and demands, perhaps of recognition and identity. All great works are statements to that effect; and only such works survive. This is why we may also accept, and state, that there are many metaphors for reality expressed differently by scientists, artists, etc. who are creators of new metaphors. They add something to our awareness of the unending possibility in the universe and in human experience. The physicist, scientist and others are doing much the same, provided the same mystical and metaphysical reality consciously works in them. These fundamental researches are what produce what we call uses of sciences, not merely the empiricism of sciences. *It is the primary quality that creates new discoveries and adds a new dimension.* Ultimately, the debate always boils down to one about symbols and the ability for communion, i.e. if not shared and experienced in isolation, it is as unverifiable and non-existent.

There is no methodology to unite all divisions, all disciplines to recreate the whole. Of course, the interrelatedness is apparent, if not transparent. The unity of thought, lifestyles exist in each age — in the world of social set-up, economics and politics. The superstructure reflects the world but not as a cause-and-effect relationship. The relationship between *That* and reflections is *acausal.* The reflections are distorted, as is social reality which is bits and patches also of Reality. All created, manifested expressions or forms have their own laws and functions also, once created, they move with their own laws.

All this suggests the interrelatedness of life for which a vision of wholeness is necessary. This cannot be a thought or a mental concept, nor to be merely experienced as a feeling. It is a state of Communion with a uniqueness all its own. That is to say there is a state of freedom existing by itself — not *from* anything. It is not devoid of responsibility, nor is it mere non-conformism. This self-expression is a statement about one's life; it is a process of self-exploration and self-definition. In this sense it is also a process of continuous definition of society provided the individual is not carried away like the raindrop, by his genius — personality — and the uniqueness of his spiritual experience become unrelated or isolated from all else. This is why society recognizes itself in authentic creative expressions also; no less are these reflected in manners, attitudes, ethics, behaviour and so on.

Once again, the debate comes from a notion of the false dichotomy of "public or private", "personal or impersonal". Nevertheless, the underlying truth is a recognition of the fact that this dichotomy is a mental construct. This is what governs all spheres of modern life including all the objectives and the pursuit of knowledge and happiness. The individual — personality — having separated one's identity from one's work, one's life from the rest of life in order to remain an individual — which in itself in isolation is the illusion, i.e. to maintain that man is outside the painting! That one — the self — is separate from life, society, science or whatever; perhaps, when this is so, this is why the personal experience of the creative person becomes a mass commodity for production also — a saleable item. Soon, creativity begins to cater to the socio-economic powers that be. When personal experience becomes a status symbol, it loses its aesthetic or higher nature. It becomes less revolutionary in nature, and conformist. It becomes reabsorbed into "thing-ness" far away from Oneness. It is not any longer self-expression, nor creative in nature.

Finally, to sum up, the particular use of the term person is different from the category of Being. In fact, even the word "individual" is rooted to mean whole, complete. In this sense, the same applies to the word "alone" — being One without a second; a total, complete individual. In turn, whole–complete is the same as holistic, implying Oneness. From this flows the idea of being holy, virtuous, and that is inseparable from the notion of beauty, goodness, love and creation. The experience of all these words may only be known within this holistic context directly — experientially — and not conceptually; that experience which has an ineffable quality of Beingness, Aliveness, Wonder, Delight. While all this refers to a numinous dimension that is totally individual or is a subjective experience, yet at the same time it has quality of being universal in nature — in rare moments — the experience of communion with the essence of life, or becoming life itself. This is why all of us fundamentally wish to commune and to relate and express *beingness*. This is often and commonly referred to — on the religious plane — as the expression of the Self or Self-experession. The Self has no tangible, empirical proof — in terms of our gross senses; or, within the structure of the old — linear — mind. The proof lies in a holistic mind. Knowing the false is knowledge. But this knowing is not conceptual. This state *to be* or *being* that *was, is,* and *will be* — always eternally. In a way, it is not knowable, it is beyond knowing and not knowing.

12

Dimensionless Space as Eternal Silence

> Words cannot describe everything. The heart's message cannot be delivered in words. If one receives words literally, he will be lost. If he tries to explain with words, he will not attain enlightenment in this life. —Saying of a Zen Master

> The Void is not of the nature of a black abyss or a bottomless pit. Rather is its nature "vast and expansive like space itself".
> It is apprehended as "serene, marvellous, and pure, brilliant and all inclusive".
> Above all does it partake of the nature of light, and is not anything.
> For Void is Mind itself, and Mind Itself is Void, That is the answer. — Chinese saying

"OBJECTIVE" truth — understanding at any given point of time — is relative. But this process of "knowing" by itself is a dead end. This given way of knowledge is part of the social system we are brought up in, wherein reasons, explanations, cause-and-effect, objectivity vs subjectivity and so on are taken to be axiomatic truths of a paradigm that arises out of a split-mind in which the vehicle of thought, communication, i.e. language itself is dualistic. Therefore, whatever the efforts, direction, mankind is making towards knowledge, truth, etc. is only futile in *the context of reaching the goals of wholeness, harmony, totality*, or whatever other various labels as are — or have been used — in different cultural subgroups (both diachronically and synchronically). What is required is a change of paradigm, a change in direction, about our very perceptions, i.e. the perspective that governs human existence today. For example, consciousness has to be apprehended individually, subjectively, yet also not so, in a way. Consciousness exists as each being, and is exactly where we are, *Here* and *Now*. It is beyond space and time, beyond cause-and-effect and other notions (Malik 1991b).

The *now* is a dimensionless point that vibrates and throbs in moments of *Now, Now*; each moment being a totality. It is not apprehended by reasons of a system that thinks dualistically, least of all in the structure of existing languages. In fact, the social system emerging from dualistic thinking covertly taboos any other perspective — especially the holistic view of knowing "who one is", "who you are", or "who I am", since this would negate all existing ways of behaviour and action and institutions (even if these claim to be reaching or achieving wholeness, harmony and peace). The current systems are limited to three-dimensional areas, whereas the total view belongs to another dimension, not necessarily a fourth one or may be *one* which is not related and does not at all arising out of the other three. The fourth dimension — we may say — includes the other three, once it is apprehended. In that space all concepts of time, space and linearity are seen, yet, not any more in the sense of what they were without the fourth. The earlier concepts of the three are now subservient, or serve the whole "mind" and reflect it. In this sense, coming from that fourth dimension, even the dualistic language becomes an instrument — vehicle — for its communication where the unsaid and unseen comes forth, beyond words (Wei 1963) (*fig*. 12.1).

The present social system is totally opposed to all such approaches. The taboo on knowing "who you are" is necessary since it is opposed to the notion of a person. The system we live in, however, is a personality-oriented one. It encourages the intrinsic existence of the little self. All civilized societies encourage this self, build institutions, write histories of their past, build memorial stones and erect monumental institutions within its framework. Even the idea of sacrificing the ego or person to a larger concept — as a tribe or nation, symbolized by a flag, or

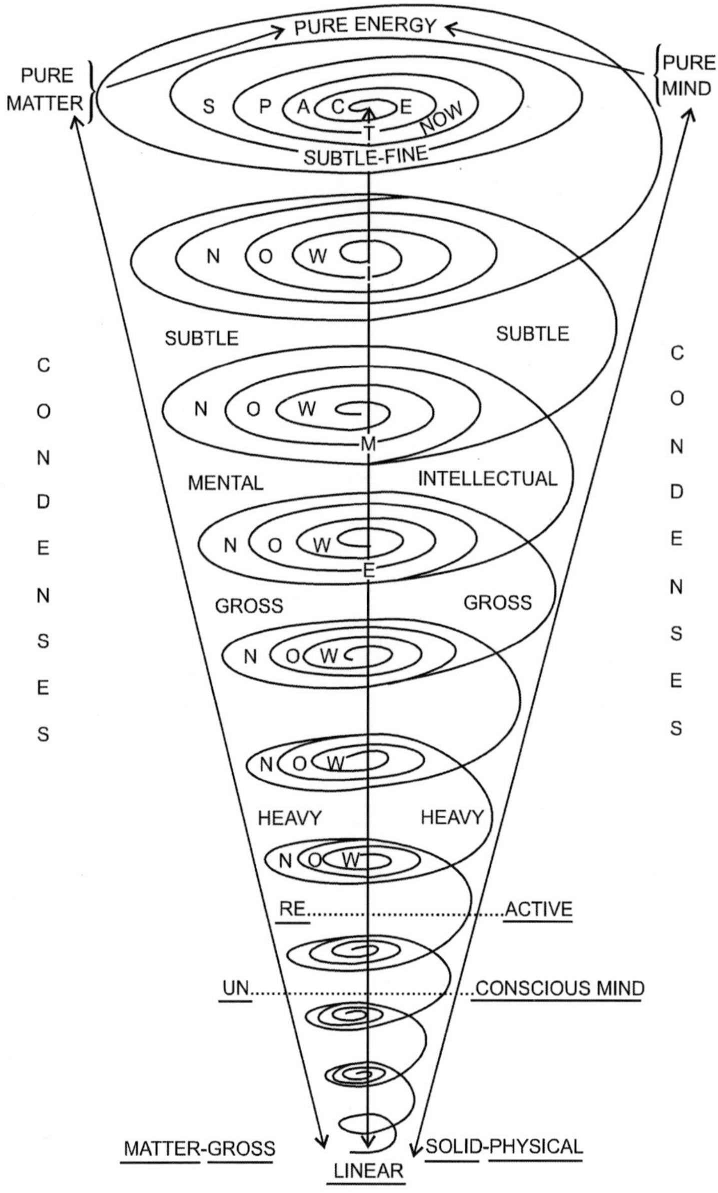

fig. 12.1: One energy

Explanation to *fig*. 12.1

In the beginning there was a void, no space, no time. Then appeared I and one whole energy system. I then got manifested as I AM, into various forms. It then stated in words I am this, I am eating, I am walking, and so on. So it is the I am that is eating and walking and so on, or I is eating, I is walking, etc. when on eliminates the AM in language. The I also has a shadow called I, the I the original one is self. However, the I, the shadow the concept begins to believe that it is the doer and knower, etc. it is like I is the power of attorney but it takes over what has been given to it by I, so infact it can do nothing, it pretends to do, and starts to believe it is this doer or knower. But this false self, this shadow, this mirage can do nothing at all. This is the confusion that mental self has to clear up by awareness, to wake up. THIS THE Clown, the me, pretending, the Great Pretender!

This pure energy, as pure mind, pure matter pure space is all One. It is very subtle and fine expressed in moments of Now. However, it begins to condense in to many levels from pure form, to subtle fine, to subtle to mental, intellectual and further gross and heavy, re-active, to the unconscious mind, to very gross solid physical and the linear thought levels. The pure energy is then covered, like the sun is covered by clouds which are not solid actually. It is also like H_2O o is water, vapours and solid ice. Nevertheless it is all H_2O whatever different names one gives it. But the word is not the "thing" it is just a symbol. In the end it all one energy, appearing as many. It is all Divinity. All God if one uses that word for that formless nameless unseen Consciousness. It is not an object, not a concept. The eye cannot see itself, except through its products. I AM what not is seen, am not the body, not name, etc. I AM THAT I AM, BE STILL AND KNOW THAT I AM. MY FATHER AND I ARE ONE.

other images — is an enhancement of the same notion since it negatively glorifies the ego. All dualistic conditioning inherently involves the notion of self and others as axiomatic, separate entities. This fundamental basis of a subject–object dichotomy is one on which entire civilizations have been created. Given this situation, can conditioned individuals of this dualistic system even "see" a dimension that is beyond all this? Will they not resist it, since it takes away the very grounds on which this self or their social system is standing? A linear split-mind, cannot even allow or see the whole, for it is beyond concepts. The "I" concept can only project concepts. Wholeness demands the total abandonment of all such current notions.

However, there is also a stage when the conceptual level of intellectual understanding within dualism is reached whereby one may be ready to take off — reptiles flying as birds in evolution into the sky leaving no traces of the steps taken in space, beyond territorial attachment in a sense. But this take-off is only a beginning, a journey into the fourth dimension where the ladder has been removed, where there is no turning back or coming down again.

Again, such understanding, or apperception of wholeness, is not objective — my understanding is valueless to you. It cannot be transferred or transmitted to you. It can only be pointed out. Phenomenally or dualistically, one may be led within "sight" but you alone can "see" it. But even this is a metaphorical statement since truth cannot be "seen". In fact, trying to look or see is in itself false. For there is nothing to "see" even in the right direction. And who is to "see", since there is nobody there? Discouraging, pessimistic?

There are words for such a dimensional space (*ākāśa*) but the meanings vary and are not easily expressive. We may, for instance, substitute for the word meditation, or *dhyāna*, or awareness — variously indicative of inner awareness, intuitive visions, spiritual awareness and so on. But whether expressed by oriental or occidental mystics it does imply "the cessation of any kind of mentation, implying a vivid state of consciousness free of all abiding discursive, mental activity by means of images, forms and figures that are produced imaginatively", as St. John of the Cross had put it. This is non-objective, impersonal awareness — beyond words, or thought of the personal self. The self-nature which even Zen masters refer to is not the personal self but the subjective total mind in the non-dual sense which is often referred to as one mind, no-mind, etc. This is a state when knowledge and wisdom are of a totally different order; now action and spontaneity implies non-action which would be labelled as ignorance from the split or linear mind's viewpoint. All that is needed is to decondition one's self, by waking up, by being conscious, for clarity to appear, and one that always was there. Why is one not at peace? Because 99.9 per cent of everything one thinks, and of most one does, is for oneself. And, there isn't one! (Wei 1963).

The most serious handicap in understanding Dimensionless Space is to start on the wrong foot. This has become the fatal most step — and the first step is the last step. That is why reading the ancient and modern wisdom of mystics is of no avail, since any statement is quickly subsumed into the conditioned dualistic notions — perhaps enthusiastically — which fits in like a personal patch work. But not in a thousand million years will this produce an essential understanding such as this inner urge is obliging us to seek. As busy bees we are adding to the stock, wasting time, for we are merely building that very *persona* whose illusory existence stands between our phenomenal selves and the truth of what we are, which is what the urge in us is seeking. Even the laying down, renunciation of everything that we consider as ours, which is ignorance — even there the self takes charge of the operation, successfully. The need is to strip oneself of all garments for only in total nakedness will that come which we seek — the whole, the indivisible which is not "ours", "theirs", or a doctrine. As long as we do not perceive the fatuity of a phenomenon convincing itself how marvellous it is, we will never come to the knowledge of that which we are and when we have understood that as a phenomenon, we are not.

What is this *now*, the total *present* (not past, present future of conceptual linear time) — this dimensionless point? That *Now* has no duration, it is not horizontal. It has only contact with seriality at right angles to it. Its measurement is within, in this timeless dimension so to speak. It is not another extension of time, it is eternally *present* in the *now*, that allows for creative *expression*. This is what links us to the other three dimensions. It is this point that cuts across space and as a concept it is spatial rather than temporal. Yet, it is not a fleeting moment; for in it exist all things potentially and as manifestations which is time, i.e. from the noumenon everything is projected. It is the invisible portal through which intuition reaches us. It is that universal or limitless interior (spatially thought of) which is all we ever were or will be and which is "out of time". It is the sole line of communication between our enveloping totality and our apparent existence as separate individual creatures. The present alone in our experience is *what is*, and phenomenally it is not: for, it is only an imaginary division in time between past and future. These are concepts that artificially divide a continuity in time and space. *Now* alone represents that we are in an apparent world in which we are not, since therein we are appearances — phenomenon only. We are nothing but as the *present*, neither existing nor not existing.

The "I" concept is like the clown in a circus who pretends to be the doer of all acts. As children we are aware of this and laugh at him, not taking the clown seriously. But as grown-ups we take the clown — the "I" — as seriously as if it "does" or "acts", or is responsible for everything. As innocent children having child-like quality, we knew better, although in both cases, we love the clown. All so-called volition is the "I" manifestation, that seeks anything, enlightenment included! Under the compulsion of the "I" concept how could anything be realized except the very enhancement of itself? It wants even pseudo-understanding, pseudo-enlightenment by which the "I" can pose as a sage since its own liquidation is not desirable. Thus every path, every analysis, every discipline must lead us away from home. For, all action is the "I" concept; there really being no actor at all. The "I" concept can do no service either, unless that concept disappears. When it does, that which we are, is there all the time. This would be the consequence of non-action, speaking in a dualistic language.

That dimensionless point, that space, is the eternal silence, more eloquent than words yet from which words appear and into which they disappear. Silence is not a negation of noise, it is a stillness — "Be still and know that I am" — the mind away from thoughts, cerebration and the like; all that act as barriers to knowing our true nature. Is there even a split-second when we are still, without random thoughts that are there constantly as chatter, as surface waves of consciousness? The space between thoughts — infinitesimal from the viewpoint of split-mind — is an indication of that space. It is a duration beyond duration since in itself it is atemporal and infinite. It is that background against which all happens, the experience of time and its accessories. That is Space, the Reality, the screen on which the ever-moving pictures of conceptual life are projected. Knowing this, its incalculable potency becomes apparent, for this is no other than whole mind.

In other words, birth is the birth of the "I" concept, and death its death. This is what projects the world for without it there is neither birth nor death. Similarly, "without", "within", "above", "below", arises out of this "I" concept, of thoughts of a split-mind. There is no resolution of those opposites, for this attempt is of the same nature, of the aggregate of latent tendencies held together by the "I" concept. How do we know all this, ephemeral nature, this transitoriness, this phenomenon? Because we are this stillness, this spaceless–timeless Present, this continuum of consciousness wherein there is the humility, truly spontaneous. For that which is — that we are — comes forth naturally. *Karma* and reincarnation are also the creations of the "I" concept, as also "mind", "matter" — words for a continuum in which consciousness is the only Subjectivity — all else being objects or concepts.

Thus, there is nothing to be acquired, only the error to be exposed. Perhaps, the readjustment is in giving up the old addiction, the disease of thinking as an "I" concept, that I am a body, a mind, a word, etc. We do need to give up the old ways. It is not only that we have to give up the "I" concept but also the "giving up" since with it, goes the reality of the cosmos, that never has been or could be; only the whole mind can reveal this as direct cognition, which makes it very obvious (Malik 1991a).

The mind in its wholeness is Silence, beyond opposites and comparisons; it is what may be called the "witness" of Vedānta, Buddha-mind of Zen, Father of Christianity. It helps escape the pendulum movement of the dualistic mind, going tic-toc, tic-toc; the interval is what we need in order to avert it. This is to be aware, to be awakened instantly — not though to be likened to any sensorial perception. The whole mind continues to know the divided mind which it considers as an aberration. But we all know it in our daily life as the consciousness which is aware of it all, ever present, ever awake — except when it misidentifies with what it sees. It is that quality of "seeing" — where there is neither the seer nor is there the seen; that is the illusion, that is the splitting into subjectivity and objectivity — only the Universal Presence knows this. Call it void, space, *ākāśa* or whatever — for conceptual language can only point in the right direction of, who am I?

I am (is) pure consciousness, I am (is) love itself. *I* neither *knows* consciousness nor *knows* love for that creates duality since the "I" concept intervenes creating things, imaginary entities. Through the false, the untruths that which is, is laid bare. Were all individuals to lose the "I" concept, the notion of a separate self, automatically nothing deriving from it would remain, i.e. pride, greed, envy, ambition and so on. While today a minority is thus free, what a difference it would make if to whatever degree we can succeed in weakening its hold, to that extent there could be space for integrated life on earth.

The Universal Presence knows no self or "I". Here, the impersonality of pure consciousness, inaccessible to the process of identification, represents the plenitude of the void, space, the one mind. In other words, since pure consciousness is *what is*, nothing else is — as I am not. There is only it, unknown to itself. Nor can it be, for there is nothing. That is why it is called dimensionless space, since there is no one to be. And the Universal Presence is at the same time Universal Absence, for there is nothing to be present and nowhere for a presence to be.

Perceiving in itself is pure consciousness, neither the perceiver, nor that which is perceived. Perceiving, witnessing, is the manifestation of pure consciousness. The rest are all concepts and interpretations. This has to be understood as an insight by the no-mind, an impersonal non-entity. And whosoever is conscious of this and nothing else, is that eternal *Now* — Space, Silence. All else, in time, is unreal. Knowing, understanding this, abolishes one. The dream vanishes, and only non-manifestation — timeless, spaceless, the immutable remains (*fig*. 12.2).

For one who knows this, even while his body flows horizontal in the stream of time as with the rest of mankind, his mind has acquired the vertical dimension at right angles from each moment of the temporal river. He is beyond the tic-toc, action–reaction, cause–effect of circumstance. Vertical vision is a consequence, not a method. He lives in that eternal silence, that space beyond words — inner or outer — which we take for granted in civilized societies where it is believed that anything can take place because of mere inner verbiage — a primary occupation. But in order to be "spaced out" — this verbiage is the biggest barrier, greatest hindrance to the development of man's spiritual possibilities.

> When he opens his mouth he is lost, when he seals his mouth he is lost. If he does not open it, if he does not seal it, he is 108,000 miles away from truth. — Another Chinese saying

fig. 12.2: Void is fullness

Explanation to *fig.* 12.2

There is this speherical spiral movement of the moments of Now. That is the context of all contexts, from the microcosm to the macrocosm. IT being all., it's a Movement of one energy system. It is like in the ocean there are all kinds of bubbles, foam, waves and so on. These form in the ocean are forming because of the inherent energy of and in the ocean, arising from the movement in the depths and other forces of gravity, the impact of moons pull and so on, that impact human, animals, plants, etc. yet these forces are not visible directly. Seeing this totality and wholeness, everything impacting everything, because of the inherent function of universal energy, everything so called thing effecting everything, everything being the cause of everything, the waves or bubble using it as a metaphor, imagines itself to be independent, autonomous and having a will of its own. But the bubble has no independent existence, this brief this short-lived existence. Knowing this, if one is aware of it all, one could laught, although until then this imaginary conceptual self feels like having anexternal existence. Amazing is the awareness of this ephemeral existence, not solid and persistent at all. It is this "me", this false conceptual "I" through this conditioning, this social creator all the mischief, this imaginary linguistic self. One gets trapped in this frivolous game. It takes time to realize that all one has to do is to remove the veils of so many false selves, notions of an as if worlds based on the non-existing body, in this linear time based on the logical left brain and not the intuitive on Higher Self. Once one knows this, this knowing is beyond words and the little thought me and I. In this "knowing" one knows that there is pure spiralling, pure energy spiralling, spherical movement of Now. This emptiness is full void in fullness, it is no-thing (think), there is neither the mind nor matter. Never mind, does not matter.

Bibliography

Bartley, Warren, 1978, *Werner Erhard: The Transformation of a Man*, New York: C.N. Potter.

Bateson, G., 1979, *Mind and Nature: A Necessary Unity*, New York: E.P. Dutton.

Bidney, David (ed.), 1980, *The Concept of Freedom in Anthropology*, The Hague: Mouton.

Bohm, David, 1980, *Wholeness and the Implicate Order*, London: Routledge.

Capra, Fritjof, 1980, *The Tao of Physics*, London: Bantam Books.

Dobzhansky, T., 1962, *Mankind Evolving: The Evolution of the Human Species*, New Haven and London: Yale University Press.

Dossey, Larry, 1982, *Space, Time and Medicine*, Boulder, CO: Sambhala.

Eliade, Mircea, 1962, *The Two and the One*, London: Harvill Press.

Hallowel, Irwing, 1960, "Self, Society and Culture in Phylogenetic Perspective", in *Evolution after Darwin*, ed. S. Tax, Chicago: University of Chicago Press.

Krishnamurti, J., 1982, *The Flight of the Eagle*, London: J. Krishnamurti Foundation.

Krishnamurti, J. and David Bohm, 1985, *The Ending of Time*, San Francisco: Harper and Row.

Kuhn, Thomas, 1970, *The Structure of Scientific Revolutions*, Chicago: University of Chicago Press.

Malik, S.C., 1968, *Indian Civilization: The Formative Period*, Shimla: Indian Institute of Advanced Study.

——— (ed.), 1971a, *Indian Civilization: The First Phase*, Shimla: Indian Institute of Advanced Study.

——— (ed.), 1971b, *Management and Organization of Indian Universities*, Shimla: Indian Institute of Advanced Study.

———, 1972, "Human Evolution: Some Reflections on Its Philosophy", *Eastern Anthropologist*, Special "Man and Society" Number, pp. 125-136.

——— (ed.), 1975, *Understanding Indian Civilization: A Framework of Enquiry*, Shimla: Indian Institute of Advanced Study.

——— (ed.), 1977a, *Dissent, Protest and Reform Movements in Indian Civilization*, Shimla: Indian Institute of Advanced Study.

——— (ed.), 1977b, Criteria of Social Status in India, Shimla: Indian Institute of Advanced Study.

———, 1978a, "New Images of the Past for a Developing Nation", in *The New Wind, Changing Identities*, ed. Kenneth David, The Hague: Mouton.

——— (ed.), 1978b, *Indian Movements: Some Aspects of Dissent, Protest and Reform*, Shimla: Indian Institute of Advanced Study.

——— (ed.), 1986, *Determinants of Social Status in India*, Shimla: Indian Institute of Advanced Study.

———, 1991a, "Pursuit of Knowledge, Creativity and Happiness", seminar on "Pursuit of Knowledge and Happiness" organized by Indian Institute of Advanced Study, Shimla, ed. R.K. Misra and B.M Sagar, pp. 130-40, New Delhi: Munshiram Manoharlal.

———, 1991b, "Dimensionless Space as Eternal Silence", seminor on "Inner and Outer Space" organized by Indira Gandhi National Centre for the Arts, pp 43-46, New Delhi: Abhinav.

Manners, Robert A. and David Kaplan (eds), 1969, *Theory in Anthropology: A Sourcebook*, London: Aldine Publishing.

Mishra, Sarlu (ed.), 1985, *The Holistic Bulletin*, II(1), New Delhi.

Morrison, Philip and Phyllis, 1982, *Powers of Ten*, San Francisco: Scientific American Books.

Muktananda, 1978, *The Play of Consciousness*, San Francisco: Harper and Row.

Nisargadatta, 1973, *I Am That*, Bombay: Chetana.

Osborne, Arthur, 1974, *The Collected Works of Ramana Maharshi*, Madras.

Papadopoullos, T., 1975, "Anthropological Criteria for a Notion of Progress", *Diogenes*, 23(91): 32-56.

Pearce, Joseph Chilton, 1981, *The Bond of Power*, London: E.P. Dutton.

Postle, Denis, 1976, *Fabric of the Universe*, London: Crown Publishing.

Prigogine, Ilya and Isabelle Stengers, 1985, *Order Out of Chaos*, New York: Flamingo.

Ramakrishna, 1980, *The Gospel of Sri Ramakrishna*, by M. Madras, Kolkatta: Sri Ramakrishna Math.

Sheldrake, R., 1983, *A New Science of Life*, London: Tarcher.

Teilhard de Chardin, P., 1959, *The Phenomenon of Man*, New York: Harper & Brothers.

Washburn, S.S. (ed.), 1961, *Social Life of Early Man*, Viking Fund Publications No. 31, Chicago.

Watts, Alan, 1972, *The Book: On the Taboo Against Knowing Who You Are*, New York: Vintage Books.

Watson, Lyall, 1980, *Life Tide: The Biology of Consciousness*, New York: Bantam Books.

Wei, Wu Wei, 1963, *Ask the Awakened: The Negative Way*, London: Routledge and Kegan Paul.

Index